# TRUTH IS
# FRAGMENTARY

Also by Gabrielle Bell:

*The Voyeurs*
*Cecil and Jordan in New York*
*Lucky*
*Lucky Vol. 2*
*When I'm Old and Other Stories*
*Gabriellebell.com*

Design by Tom Kaczynski
Copy Editing by Cassidy Wilson

Uncivilized Books
P. O. Box 6534
Minneapolis, MN 55406
USA
uncivilizedbooks.com

First Edition, June 2014

10  9  8  7  6  5  4  3  2  1

ISBN 978-0-9889014-5-2

DISTRIBUTED TO THE TRADE BY:
Consortium Book Sales & Distribution, LLC.
34 Thirteenth Avenue NE, Suite 101
Minneapolis, MN 55413-1007
cbsd.com
Orders: (800) 283-3572

Printed in Hong Kong

GABRIELLE BELL

# TRUTH IS FRAGMENTARY

## TRAVELOGUES & DIARIES

UNCIVILIZED BOOKS, PUBLISHER

# TABLE OF CONTENTS

# So what is this thing, anyway?

This is a collection of comic diaries I kept between the years of 2010 & 2013, when I was invited to attend several international comic festivals. As a struggling, obscure cartoonist, these festivals were important to me. They gave me an opportunity to travel to places I never would have been able to afford, much less have a reason to visit. They also gave me the validation and identity as a "professional artist" that I badly craved. Finally, they provided me a chance to "get out of my shell" and meet other artists. It was for these reasons that I felt compelled to keep comic diaries of the trips and post them on my blog. It was a part of my life that seemed more meaningful than the rest, a dream that had come true.

When a diary is public, it becomes a different thing. You no longer do it for yourself, you do it for us, the readers. Your life and self become "material," and you learn to take yourself less seriously. You make yourself accountable. And then, when you find yourself editing and rewriting and twisting the truth here and there, and even living life differently than you ordinarily would in order to serve the "story," is it even a diary anymore? According to *Webster's Encyclopedic Unabridged Dictionary*, it is now a journal. But according to Wikipedia, "journalistic integrity is based on the principles of truth, accuracy, and factual knowledge." So I can't call myself a journalist, either. For that matter, a travel diary is not actually a travelogue, which is (according to *Webster's*) "a lecture describing travels, usually illustrated by photographs, exhibited items, etc." For all practical purposes, let's just call it a diary.

It was hard to carve out chunks of time for the diary on those trips while running around meeting people and figuring out where I was supposed to be. Comic creation is a cumbersome thing and requires a good deal of concentration. The only time I had to reflect and focus was when I was on the plane, usually en route to the destination, since I would be too burned out on the way back.

That is why I started the annual July Diary, a month-long comic diary of my daily life. It was, after all, the experience of being myself in the world that interested me. Where or when it was happening was not exactly immaterial, but any experience would do.

I did these comics for myself, of course, but I did them just as much for you, dear reader. I offer up my insecurities, my boorishness, my vanity, and my hundreds of mistakes for your scrutiny and judgment. It is humiliating to expose myself this way, but it is worse to try to hide. At the very least, they are good for a laugh, with me or at me, take your pick.

Gabrielle Bell, 3/4/2014

Small Press Expo, Stockholm, Sweden,
April 24th - 25,th 2010

april 22nd, 2010

At the airport. This is an experiment. I'm going to publish this scratchy thing as is. I'm all alone at the food court, yet I feel all eyes watching me as I write these words.

Actually, since I started doing that last panel, MK joined me. She lent me this nice pen, because the one I brought is too fat. MK didn't get much sleep last night. We are super early because we anticipated craziness.

ARE WE SITTING NEXT TO EACH OTHER?

HMM?

DO WE HAVE SEATS NEXT TO EACH OTHER?

I DON'T KNOW.

SORRY.

And... that's about it. Next to us is a group of Swedes, maybe delayed because of the volcano ash from Elijasnadofoluh. I made up that spelling because I don't have the internet on hand.

And... this man has been yelling into his phone for quite some time.

ALLO? JON!? IT'S ME! I'M AT KENNEDY AIRPORT !!!

WHEN he saw me staring at him he turned his chair around the other way

I just love this man here though this drawing is pointless in that it doesn't ~~portray~~ capture his stuffiness or charming nebbish-ness or whatever it is I like about him.

SBARRO

and I've already developed a crush on this janitor, who I think is slightly mentally challenged. Actually, I bet he has some amazing thing he invented in his room that could tremendously benefit mankind, or has discovered a cure for cancer but no one will listen to him.

9

And I love to walk around the airport, looking at books & magazines. Every time I catch myself in the mirror I straighten my posture.

I swear, if they just put mirrors up every where, on every building, on every corner, I would never slouch, I— what's that? My pants? Oh, why, thank you! I'm very proud of them.

I bought them for two dollars at a thrift store. They were huge and shapeless, and I sewed them up last night to be form-fitting. I even managed to make them "boot cut." Huh? Nope, never had a lesson, just figured it out myself. Of course, my closet is full of not-so-successful fashion projects.

Now I'm on the plane and that's why my drawing is even worse now. It's dark & hard to see. I have to go pee for the third time and don't want to bother MK again, who is watching Fantastic Mr. Fox.

april 23rd | Now I'm sitting here in the dining room of the Arthotel in Stockholm. That there is Ron across from me.

THEY'RE BRINGING ME ON A TRAIN TO COPENHAGEN! I'M ACTUALLY EXCITED ABOUT THAT. FIVE HOURS, BEAUTIFUL SCENERY. I'M SORRY, AM I BABBLING?

THAT'S WHY I CAME HERE, FOR YOUR BABBLING.

And now Tom Gauld, Shannon O'Leary & MK have joined us.

NOW, HOW DO I DO THIS? I PUT IT IN HERE AND CRACK IT LIKE THIS?

ASK GABRIELLE. SHE'S AN EXPERT.

WHAT'RE YOU DRAWING THERE?

BACK TO HAVING MY LIFE DOCUMENTED.

Because see earlier we had breakfast here with Mk & Paul Gravett.

I'M SO HAPPY THEY'VE GOT SOFT-BOILED EGGS! I'VE BEEN EATING THEM FOR THE PAST TWO WEEKS.

YOU *HAVE*?

YES, SOMETIMES I HAVE THEM FOR DINNER TOO. THEY ARE SO PERFECT AND ROUND AND SIMPLE.

ALL OTHER FOOD IS SO COMPLICATED.

ARE YOU EGG BOUND?

All morning other Americans from the festival came & went. I've been drawing this comic this whole time.

DO YOU THINK THIS WORK IS TOO SLOPPY TO PUT ON THE INTERNET?

NO

BUT IT'S SO DISPROPORTIONATE AND NONSENSICAL... ...I AM NOW JUST FISHING FOR COMPLIMENTS.

HOW CAN I GIVE YOU A COMPLIMENT IF YOU WON'T LET ME READ IT?

THEY HAVE CAVIAR IN A TUBE HERE.

IS IT GOOD?

IT'S OKAY.

Well, now that I'm all caught up on the goings on here I'll work backward. MK and ~~the rest~~ I changed planes in Amsterdam and on the next plane I met Franz, a retired sea captain on his way back from China.

I WAS THERE IN THE EARTHQUAKE AND THEN I HAD FOOD POISONING FOR THREE DAYS. I HAD A CABLE GOING IN AND ONE GOING OUT.

SO THIS VOLCANO SEEMS LIKE NO BIG DEAL.

He told me a joke:

SO A FRENCH YOUNG WOMAN GOES TO AMERICA TO JOIN HER NEW HUSBAND OUT IN THE COUNTRYSIDE. THEN HE FALLS INTO A BEAR TRAP AND GETS GANGRENE AND HAS TO GET HIS FOOT AMPUTATED. SO THE YOUNG WIFE CALLS HER MAMA AND SAYS, OH, MAMA, IT'S TERRIBLE, MY HUSBAND ONLY HAS ONE FOOT. (DO YOU SAY ONE FOOT OR ONE FEET?)

FOOT

AND HER MAMA SAYS, DON'T WORRY, DEAR, YOUR FATHER ONLY HAS SIX INCHES AND WE GET ALONG FINE.

april 26th Monday — Well, I went straight from the first day of this trip to the last... I have failed my real-time documentation experiment. I find that after spending time with a lot of people for an extended period of time, my ability to think is greatly impaired. I really tried to keep this diary, but every time I picked it up I had to put it down five minutes later and the next time I picked it up I'd have forgotten what I'd intended to write & then I'd have to put it down again.

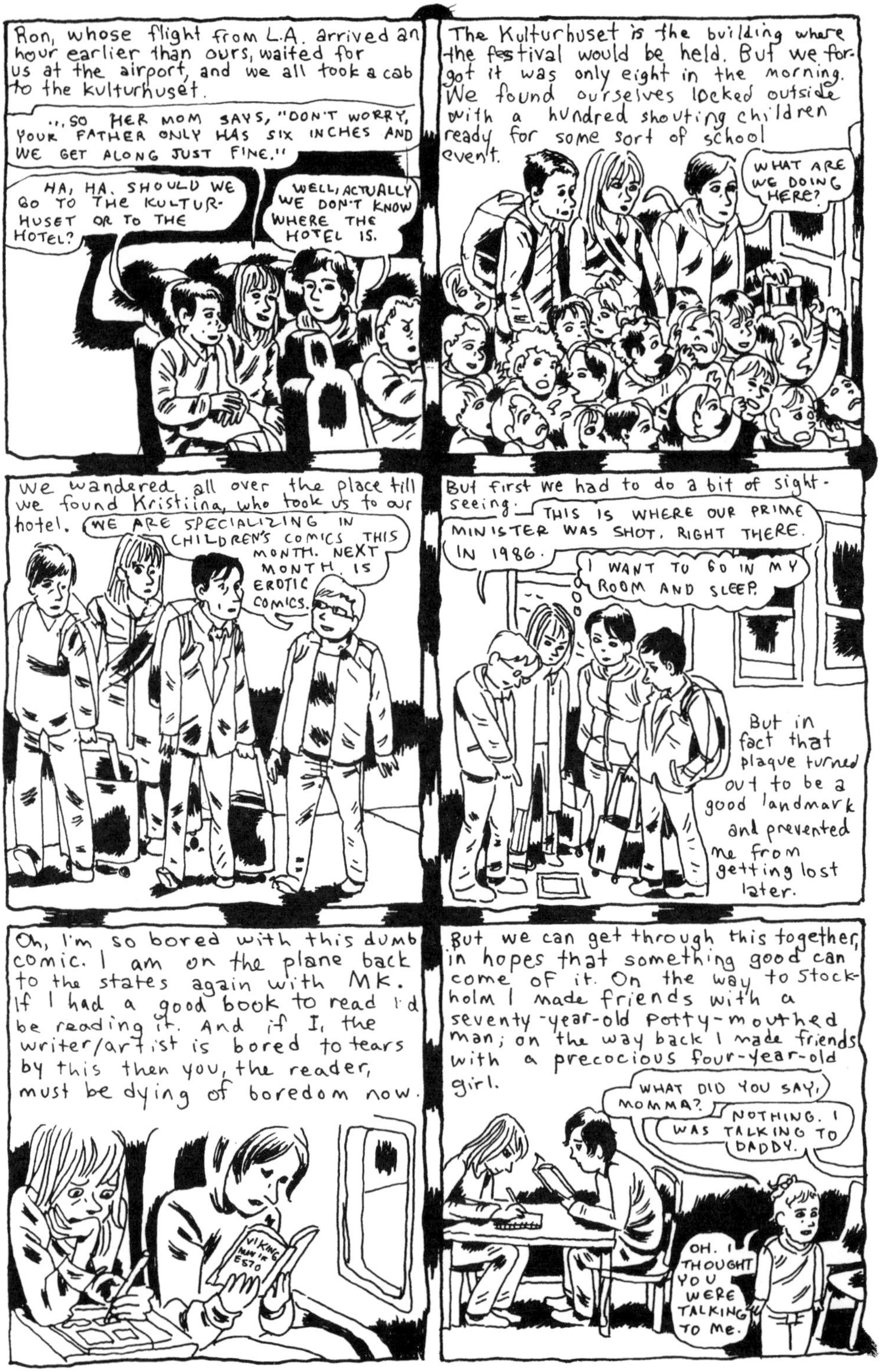
Ron, whose flight from L.A. arrived an hour earlier than ours, waited for us at the airport, and we all took a cab to the kulturhuset.
...SO HER MOM SAYS, "DON'T WORRY, YOUR FATHER ONLY HAS SIX INCHES AND WE GET ALONG JUST FINE."
HA, HA. SHOULD WE GO TO THE KULTURHUSET OR TO THE HOTEL?
WELL, ACTUALLY WE DON'T KNOW WHERE THE HOTEL IS.
The Kulturhuset is the building where the festival would be held. But we forgot it was only eight in the morning. We found ourselves locked outside with a hundred shouting children ready for some sort of school event.
WHAT ARE WE DOING HERE?
We wandered all over the place till we found Kristiina, who took us to our hotel.
WE ARE SPECIALIZING IN CHILDREN'S COMICS THIS MONTH. NEXT MONTH IS EROTIC COMICS.
But first we had to do a bit of sightseeing.
THIS IS WHERE OUR PRIME MINISTER WAS SHOT. RIGHT THERE. IN 1986.
I WANT TO GO IN MY ROOM AND SLEEP.
But in fact that plaque turned out to be a good landmark and prevented me from getting lost later.
Oh, I'm so bored with this dumb comic. I am on the plane back to the states again with MK. If I had a good book to read I'd be reading it. And if I, the writer/artist is bored to tears by this then you, the reader, must be dying of boredom now.
VIKING MAY IF ES70
But we can get through this together, in hopes that something good can come of it. On the way to Stockholm I made friends with a seventy-year-old potty-mouthed man; on the way back I made friends with a precocious four-year-old girl.
WHAT DID YOU SAY, MOMMA?
NOTHING. I WAS TALKING TO DADDY.
OH. I THOUGHT YOU WERE TALKING TO ME.

She came up and stared with unabashed curiosity.

I gave her some paper & pens and I drew her. She imitated me, looking up at me and back down at the paper back and forth, carefully scribbling. Eventually her parents joined her.

WHAT'S YOUR NAME?

LOLALOLULS.

HUH?

NORA JOAN SCHULTZ. I SHOULD FIX YOUR HAIR A BIT IF YOU'RE BEING DRAWN.

Just as I was writing/drawing that, I looked up and saw her peeking through the curtain into business elite, studying the airlines' crass and blatant class system.

Meanwhile, this professional clown started talking to me.

THIS IS WHAT I DO. LOOK, THIS IS ME.

OH, WOW.

On her way back to her seat, Nora recognized me. OH, HELLO! I'M JUST GOING TO NEW YORK. MY BROTHERS AND SISTER LIVE IN NEW YORK, AND I, IN UTRECHT.

OH, REALLY?

I introduced her to the clown behind me and she repeatedly looked up and down at the photo of him trying to connect the two.

SEE THAT GUY THERE? THAT'S HIM.

Next thing I knew, they were best friends.

She proceeded to work her way down the aisle. Everyone wanted a piece of her. That girl is going to be a major force in the world some day. Just google "Nora Joan Schultz" in thirty years.

**APRIL 22ND** Okay, okay, I know you want to hear about the festival and Stockholm... It's just that it's all a blur... It began on Thursday when there was a party somewhere in the city but Ron and I, not knowing the address, just basically wandered around looking for it..

THIS IS WHERE THEY GIVE OUT THE NOBEL PEACE PRIZE.

REALLY?!

WELL, IT COULD BE.

Friday we were moved from the ArtHotel to a swank hotel out in the suburbs. I feel the extravagant breakfast buffet must be mentioned. There was every possible thing to eat that you could imagine, as much as you want. You could have a teaspoon of each thing and it'd add up to an unliftable platter.

I started the habit-initially ridiculed, but ultimately emulated-of making sandwiches for lunch later and smuggling them out. Let me tell you, to eat and travel in Sweden is very expensive.

HELLO! HUNGRY?

OH, SHOOT. I WAS HOPING NOT TO SEE ANYONE WE KNEW

GUY Delisle.

Okay, here we are, six pages into the story, sitting at the festival, selling books. Happy?

The highlight of the festival was the feminist comics panel. The big hall was filled to the brim with women and a handful of men to see Liv Strömquist, Sara Grener and the rest of us.

Liv Strömquist:
I ATTENDED A LECTURE WITH MY SISTER BY THE FEMINIST SOCIOLOGIST CARIN HOLMBERG. SHE DREW A CIRCLE AND SAID, "THIS IS SOCIETY. NOW WE'LL PUT OUR FEMINIST GLASSES ON AND LOOK AT IT FROM A FEMINIST ANGLE." WHEN SHE WROTE "PATRIARCHY" ON THE BOARD AND EXPLAINED WHAT IT WAS, IT WAS THE FIRST TIME I'D HEARD THE WORD.

WHEN I WAS SEVENTEEN,

Joanna Frojola · Sara Grenér

Shannon Leary · Liv Strömquist · Paul Gravett · Johanna Hellgren

We Americans, on the other hand, can't seem to get past talking **about** talking about feminism.

IN THE STATES FEMINISM IS KIND OF A DIRTY WORD. ONLY TWENTY PERCENT OF WOMEN ARE WILLING TO CALL THEMSELVES THAT.

YEAH, IT'S LIKE WE DON'T WANT TO COME OFF AS ANGRY OR SHRILL.

BUT I WAS VERY INSPIRED BY THE RIOT GRRRL MOVEMENT IN THE STATES IN THE NINETIES, THE D.I.Y. MOVEMENT, BIKINI KILL...

I felt sorry for Paul, who served as moderator and token patriarch.

MOVING ALONG THEN, WE'RE JUST ABOUT OUT OF TIME—

EXCUSE ME, CAN YOU STOP INTERRUPTING THEM?

And... that's about it. Not much else. There was a party that night and Austin English introduced me to Coco Moodysson.

WE SHOULD LEAVE BEFORE WE MISS THE LAST TRAIN AND HAVE TO TAKE A CAB BACK TO THE HOTEL.

HEY GABRIELLE, YOU HAVE TO COME AND MEET COCO!

I don't remember what all Coco and I talked about, but time stood still.

EVERYONE HERE IS SO NICE!

OH, THAT'S JUST BECAUSE YOU'RE AMERICAN. THEY LOVE AMERICANS HERE. YOU'RE LIKE THE KINGS OF THE WORLD.

YOU SHOULD PUT OUT A COMIC IN ENGLISH. YOU'D BE SO POPULAR IN THE STATES. OF COURSE, YOU STILL HAVE THE DISADVANTAGE OF BEING A WOMAN...

Of course, we took a cab back.

Sunday, May 25th | I don't remember any-thing at all about Sunday except we went to visit Austin, who moved from the states to live in a sweet little studio with Clara Johansson. Somehow we all managed to fit and enjoy ourselves.

Monday, May 26th | I went to Konstfack to be an opponent. Konstfack is the school of art and design in Stockholm, and an opponent is some sort of visiting mentor for a student. My student was the talented Rui Tenreiro. We had to sit and discuss his work in front of the class. For two shy people it could've been disastrous but luckily I am full of opinions just clamoring to be expressed.

I WANT TO SEE MORE **BLOOD** IN YOUR STORY, MORE **ACTION**, MORE **IN-TRIGUE**. DON'T BE AFRAID TO BE PERSONAL!

While the other Americans went to the Vasa Museum to see the 17th century ship that sank on its maiden voyage ala the Titanic, I went with Johannes to the Galago Office to scan this comic.

WAIT, SO IS IT ONE OF THOSE SHIPS WITH ALL THE OARS THAT ALL THE GUYS ROW?

WHAT, YOU THINK EVERY SCANDI-NAVIAN SHIP IS A VIKING LONG BOAT?

I MESSED UP HERE, I'VE GOTTA RE-SCAN THIS.

Tuesday, May 27th Everyone else had left. I made a big Dagwood sandwich to smuggle onto the plane for MK and me.

The flight got pretty scary when it came to our landing. The wind was pushing us sideways, and the pilot sounded terrified.

THIS IS YOUR CAPTAIN AGAIN JUST REMINDING YOU FOR THE LOVE OF GOD PLEASE MAKE SURE YOUR SEATBELT IS SECURE.

We landed with a terrible sideways bounce, and when we were safely on the ground everyone cheered. MK and I could not acknowledge the situation to each other until it was over.

WAS IT JUST ME OR DID THE PILOT SOUND LIKE HE WAS ON THE VERGE OF TEARS?

NO, HE DID.

And that is how my trip to Stockholm ended.

DO I HAVE TO DECLARE THIS EGG?

CUSTOMS →

La Comédie du Livre, Montpellier, France,
May 28th-30th 2010

May 27 2010

I am on an airplane, going to France this time. This is an enormous plane, a metropolis. We are still on the tarmac. I think we are too big to get off the ground. It's rumbling & shaking.

over there is Nicolas. He is going to Montpellier as well but we have both agreed that we like to travel alone.

And now we are up! I don't want to do this dumb comic. I want to watch "It's complicated" and have my chicken fricasee, vegetable medley & mashed potatoes with chives. But I gotta do this stupid dumb ass comic if I want to call myself a cartoonist.

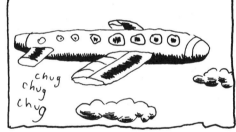

chug
chug
chug

Oh look, I am almost half done with this page. I also want to watch the episodes of The Simpsons and Bored to Death they have featured on this flight but first I must finish this page!

Okay. It is time for me to stop being so careless and write and draw neatly. And to have something to say. Like today I had lunch with Tom Hart, Leela Corman, Vanessa Davis, Karen Sneider and (introducing) Rosalee Lightning. Imagine, five cartoonists and a baby.

DO YOU WANT ONE OF YOUR OWN, GABRIELLE?

OH, I HATE BABIES.

Actually, when I get around babies, I react the same way most women my age probably do: I have the urge to give up everything and steal it away to raise as my own far away from here. I am told this is because of oxytocin.

I learned about oxytocin from a book I listened to lately called Why Women Have Sex (turns out for all the reasons you'd expect). There was a study about these animals- the mountain voles, who have an oxytocin deficit, & the prairie voles (I have no idea what they look like—there's no internet here).

anyway, the mountain voles are a promiscuous lot who abandon their children and live a wild, free-wheeling life (both males & females) while the prairie voles are a faithful, monogamous bunch who do right by their children and lead a retiring life.

HOME SWEET HOME

drink PUNCH! WAH!

So I kind of thought maybe I lack oxytocin and take after the mountain vole. But Tom & Leela were saying:

IT'S RELEASED WHEN YOU HAVE AN ORGASM - AND IT'S FOUND IN CHOCOLATE - AND WHEN YOU GIVE BIRTH.

and I realized that everyone's oxytocin level is probably affected by their environment.

anyway, I'm getting sloppy again, and let me tell you why: It's very dark here, and I'm writing this by the light of my personal TV screen, because every time I turn on the light these two prairie voles sitting two seats down from me glare.

Holding my notebook up to my chest like a violin

I guess it's time for IT'S complicated.

May 28: I'm thinking that those prairie & mountain voles would make a great comic. It's obvious: There's a romance between a prairie vole & a mountain vole: big scandal. Obviously a heart is broken. Now I'm going to picture the voles to look like care bears.

I am in my hotel room now. There's no free internet here. Otherwise I'd be googling voles. But why should I pay for internet when I can use my imagination for free? But if I had internet perhaps I could also google-image-search care-bears.

I have to tell you about my second scary landing. The wind was blowing us around terribly. It felt like we were inside a badly folded paper airplane. Or a moth. We were just fluttering around like that and I wondered how we'd ever manage to land safely.

Everyone was peeking at each other, trying to gauge whether anyone else was worried. I was reading the same paragraph of my book over & over, and I noticed the woman across from me had given up on hers entirely.

We were going very, very fast, and just before we were about to touch down we suddenly pulled back up again and flew out over the sea.

I thought about this story Ron told me about his friend Steve. Back in the eighties he was on a plane and found a channel on his headset where he could listen to the pilot in the cockpit.

THERE'S SOMETHING WRONG! I CAN'T GET THE LANDING GEAR TO WORK!

Steve was the only passenger privy to a major emergency happening on the plane.

SOMETHING IS STUCK! I DON'T KNOW WHAT'S GOING ON DOWN THERE!

FLY OVER THE CONTROL TOWER HERE. I WILL LOOK UP OUT THE WINDOW AND SEE IF I CAN SEE ANYTHING.

THAT'S YOUR PLAN?

LET ME KNOW IF YOU HAVE A BETTER IDEA!

WHAT'S GOING ON?

... IT LOOKS LIKE THE WHEELS ARE STUCK HALFWAY! MY GOD! WHAT ARE WE GOING TO DO?!

OH, SHIT, I DON'T KNOW IF THERE'S ANYTHING WE CAN DO!

Steve heard them say there was nothing to do but crash, but first they had to go out over the sea to dump out the fuel so they wouldn't explode when they hit the ground.

Meanwhile they covered the runway with some sort of giant foam covering. I asked my friend Sadie, who is studying for her commercial pilot's license, about this but she'd never heard of it.

Nobody got hurt, but Steve has never flown again. When he visits his parents back east he drives across the country.

So I was thinking about that and I felt like one of those mice you find stuck on a sticky trap, its doomed little heart pounding so hard you can see it.

I was convinced we were all going to die and was shaking visibly. I wanted to hold the hand of the man next to me, but he wasn't even holding his wife's, who was on the other side of him. If I were them I'd've been all over each other. I thought, if I had a hand to hold I'd be 90% less scared.

Of course, everything was fine. What, you think I'm writing this from the grave? In the south of France, like in southern California, it seems imposs-ible to think about death.

Pete Fromm writer

SO HOW ARE YOU? DID YOU HAVE A GOOD FLIGHT?

OH, YES, IT WAS VERY NICE.

festival organizer

(isabelle)

With just a couple hours to clean up, we went to an exhibition for Tim Sale and me. My very first art show, and it's in France, with the guy who draws Batman!

COMICS in Comédie TIM SALE GABRIELLE BELL

(GANG OF AMERICAN WRITERS)

(& cartoonists)

But I was so tired I couldn't speak. A woman asked me to sign & draw in her copy of my book, and I spent the entire time drawing an elaborate sequence of three stages of a girl turning into a chair. I don't think it was that good.

DÉSOLÉE... JE N'AI PAS DORS. *

AH.

* Sorry, I have not sleep.

Afterwards we had an "informal" meal, which could easily have made a nice wedding dinner.

(the sea)
%H₂O
cheeses
white wine
RED wine
FRUITS
OUT doors
INDIVIDUAL CRÈME CAKES w/FRUIT
LIL' BREADS
STEAK
N' MORE
A lot of cylindrical delights
orchid on table
smoked salmon
SAVORY PASTRIES
STUFFED PLUM TOMATOES
COUSCOUS salad
Little asparagus

I liked talking to Tim Sale and hearing about the "other side" of comics.

I'LL DO COMMISSIONED DRAW-INGS WHERE THEY TAKE A NUMBER SO THEY DON'T HAVE TO WAIT IN LINE AND I DRAW ANYTHING THEY WANT IN TEN MINUTES. I USUALLY CHARGE A HUNDRED OR A HUNDRED-FIFTY. OF COURSE THEY USUALLY WANT BATMAN...

100$ PER 10 MINS x 6 HOURS = $$$

I thought, I could do that!. I'll learn to draw Batman, and then I'll get rich! But then I realized that to understand how to draw Batman I'd have to learn to draw Bruce Wayne and I'd have to understand the whole story and read a lot of comic books and go in a whole other direction in my work that I wouldn't want to go in, which is the case with most of my money-making schemes.

That night & the nights thereafter, I was visited by the most terrible insomnia. For seven hours I lay there breathing, focusing every ounce of attention on trying to make myself sleep. I finally succeeded about an hour before it was time to get up. I'd like to think I reached higher levels of concentration on those nights, but it's hard to measure such things.

**Friday May 28th** I have to say, my French is just terrible. Awful. Embarrassing. Maybe this is because I'm pretty much both self-taught, and a bad student. Or it could be that I'm so shy and anxious that my mind goes blank every time I talk to anyone I don't know. But I try all the same.

JE PENSE QUE APPRENDRE PARLER JAPONAIS EST PLUS FACILE QUE PARLER FRANÇAIS.*

pierre Duba

\* I THINK THAT IT IS MORE EASY TO LEARN TO SPEAK JAPANESE THAN TO SPEAK FRENCH.

PARCE QUE.... EN JAPAN, QUAND J'ESSAYE PARLER JAPONAIS, ILS DIT:

YAY!!!

ET QUAND J'ESSAYE PARLER EN FRANÇAIS, ILS EST:

CLAP !!! CLAP !!! CLAP !!!

–BECAUSE IN JAPAN WHEN I TRY TO SPEAK JAPANESE THEY SAID:

–AND WHEN I TRY TO SPEAK FRENCH THEY IS:

OH!

YAY!!!

CLAP!CLAP!CLAP!

-I'M STÉPHANE.
-SORRY I SPEAK NOT IN FRENCH, BUT IF YOU TO SPEAK SLOWLY I CAN TO UNDERSTAND.
-AH, YOU MAKE COMICS?.
-YES, YOU LIKE THE COMICS?
-YES BUT I PREFER NOVELS.
- ME TOO! WHICH BOOKS IS YOU LIKE?

- I LIKE STEPHEN KING.
- ME TOO!
- AND I LIKE SAPPHIRE. DO YOU KNOW OF HER?
- YES, YES.
- SHE LIVES IN NEW YORK.
- I ALSO LIVE IN NEW YORK.
- I'VE NEVER LEFT MONTPELLIER. EXCEPT ONE TIME I WENT TO NANTES.
- YOU GREW UP HERE?
- YES.

I have to apologize for the way I've depicted everyone. My memory isn't so good and I couldn't find much on Google.

ME, TOO, I CAN ONLY DO ONE THING.

IT'S BECAUSE I'M NOT "THERE." I'M PRESENT WHEN I'M WORKING OR WHEN I'M THINKING ABOUT MY WORK. BUT MOST OF THE TIME I'M JUST NOT THERE. DO YOU KNOW WHAT I MEAN?

YES! BUT ARE YOU HERE, NOW? YES,

On Saturday all my books sold out so I had Sunday off. Did I go to the beach? Did I practice my French with local Frenchmen? Did I sit at a cafe? Did I say hi to Lewis Trondheim or Guy Delisle, who had been in the same booth as me? Did I even draw any comics? NO! I spazzed out in my hotel room and continued my four day no-sleep marathon.

The next morning I bought some Almond Croissants, still warm, from a fancy boulangerie and packed them in a Kleenex box because I asked Tony:

IS THERE ANYTHING SPECIAL YOU'D LIKE FROM FRANCE?

AN ALMOND CROISSANT.

I CARRIED THEM ON MY LAP ALL THE WAY.

And Tony picked me up at JFK, after a day at the beach with his friends Layla and Jordann.

THERE WAS A LOT GOING ON THERE. PEOPLE WERE DOING ACROBATICS IN THE SAND.

THEY FORMED A HUMAN CUBE

WE BURIED MARYBETH.

WE MADE SAND BREASTS ON HER.

SHE LIKED THAT.

DID YOU JUST LEAVE HER THERE?

July 2011

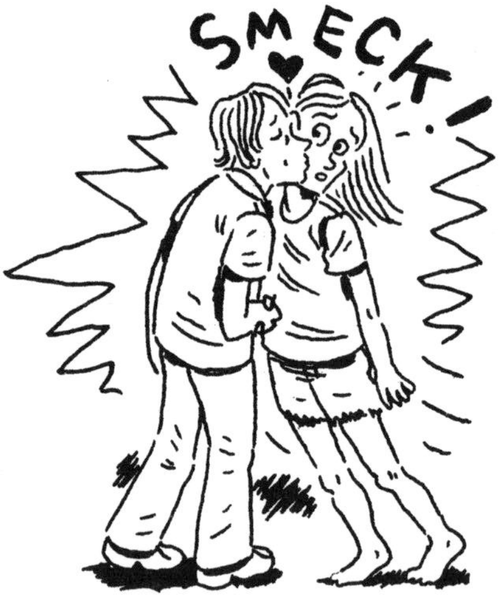
SMECK!

Friday, July first, 2011

I wore my fancy dress around the apartment, doing chores and drawing comics.

WHO IS THAT PRETTY GIRL?

WHY...IT'S ME!

I've had this dress since I was sixteen but I've only worn it in public three times. The last time was to a cotillion in 2006.

WHAT IS A COTILLION?

The time before that was during a heatwave in 2004. I changed out of it after fifteen minutes when some guy said:

I WISH I HAD A PRETTY SUMMER DRESS TO WEAR TOO.

The first time I wore the dress I was sixteen and with Sadie. We were doing some sort of impromptu street theatre where I was a bag lady with delusions of grandeur and Sadie was a masochistic street urchin who thought she was my dog.

BEAT ME?

NOT NOW, SCRUFFY! WE ARE GOING TO THE ALGONQUIN HOTEL WHERE I WILL BE DISCOVERED!

At the end of the day I changed into my leopard print capris to go to a bar and have a pizza and beer, alone.

BUT. Sadie herself intercepted and invited me over for sandwiches.

NICE PANTS.

THANKS.

## Saturday, July second

I woke up super late because I use the alarm clock on my phone which died in the night.

OH MY GOD IT IS NOTHING O CLOCK!!!

Not having a phone is disturbing.

WHAT DO I DO WHAT DO I DO? I'M SURE ALL THE PEOPLE WHO NEVER CALL ME ARE TRYING TO CALL ME NOW!

I'LL CALL TONY! HE'LL KNOW WHAT TO DO!

In fact I just want to barricade my apartment from the outside world and live here quietly until I die.

IRREVERSIBLE CLIMATE CHANGE

HATE CRIME

CATASTROPHE

WAR

(OLD FASHIONED RADIO)

But I can't, because my new room-mate Tim is moving in.

THIS IS CLAYTON. HE'S HELPING ME OUT.

HI.

HI.

Clayton moved in for one of those latin-style kiss-greetings.

SMECK!

What a disorienting day!

## Sunday, July third

Met Lizz Hickey to work on the flyer for our Desert Island mini-comics party.

ARE YOU OKAY? YOU'RE ALL WET AND DISHEVELED!

IT'S HALF RAIN AND HALF SWEAT.

I just asked Lizz to do this event with me as an excuse to collaborate with her.

I HAVE AN IDEA: YOU DRAW ME AND I DRAW YOU WEARING PARTY DRESSES AND IN THE BACKGROUND WE'LL HAVE ALL OUR CHARACTERS MINGLING WITH EACH OTHER.

YEAH GIRL!

I AM DRAWING YOU AS A FAIRY PRINCESS.

I AM SKANKIN' YOU UP LIKE A TOTAL HO.

AW, YOURS IS SO MUCH BETTER! I GOTTA GO HOME AND REDO MINE SEVERAL MORE TIMES.

ARE YOU CRAZY.

OH WELL, THE CONTRAST IS GOOD.

WHAT'S IT LIKE BEING MARRIED NOW?

IT'S CRAZY! I FEEL LIKE I'M IN A SITCOM ALL THE TIME.

I'LL COME OVER AND BE YOUR LAUGH-TRACK.

We went to Desert Island to show the flyer to Gabe.

HERE'S WHAT WE'VE GOT!

LOOKS GOOD.

HE LIKES IT!

JUST SO YOU KNOW, YOU DON'T NEED MY APPROVAL ON THIS.

AW.

# Monday, July fourth

Fourth of July. As much as I don't really like holidays, I like even less to feel left out.

I WISH I HAD AN ENGLISH BOYFRIEND JUST SO I COULD DUMP HIM TODAY TO DECLARE MY INDEPENDENCE!

HA HA

HA

For some reason I felt like a big, inert, defenseless slug while everyone bantered around me. I felt spongy and porous, like any effort to contribute to the conversation would collapse in on itself, with no shell to brace myself on.

MAYBE IF I DRINK MORE I'LL FEEL ENGAGED?

UGH. CAN'T REACH BEER. NEVER MIND.

So I just sat there, sluglike, absorbing conversational tidbits such as:

- SELZER MAY NOT BE GOOD FOR YOU BECAUSE IT DEPLETES CALCIUM.

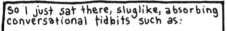

- PLANKING IS A THING WHERE YOU LAY FLAT IN WEIRD PLACES AND SOMEONE TAKES A PICTURE OF YOU AND PUTS IT ON THE INTERNET.

(AS DEMONSTRATED BY TALENTED PLANKIST DOMITILLE COLLARDEY) →

- AFTER HIS DEATH, AN ENORMOUS WOODEN DILDO WAS FOUND IN THE BATHROOM WALL OF BENJAMIN FRANKLIN'S HOUSE.

Julia and I decided we'd just as well do without fireworks.

IT'S PROBABLY ALL LOUD AND CROWDED WITH STRANGERS UP THERE ON THE ROOF.

YEAH, I'M NOT IN THE MOOD.

But when the time came:

WAIT FOR ME! I'VE GOTTA PUT MY SHOES ON!

HURRY UP! THEY'RE STARTING ALREADY!

If good sex is supposed to feel like fireworks, why don't good fireworks feel like sex?

OOOOOOOOH!

AAAAAAAAAH!

HOW COME I'M NOT FEELING ANYTHING?

# Tuesday, July fifth

Why oh why did I start this awful 31 day comic? What was I thinking?! It's like day 5!! I have **26** more comics to draw!!! As if I don't already have enough shit to do!!!

Neglected graphic novel
Neglected kramers ergot story
Neglected other book
Neglected life

Yesterday I did exactly what I should've known I'd do: Instead of taking the two hours I'd alloted myself, I spent pretty much all day on my comic, taking plenty of breaks and checking the internet often.

HEE, HEE, BENJAMIN FRANKLIN'S DILDO!

THIS IS GOOD MATERIAL! I CAN'T JUST DASH THIS STUFF OFF!

I got the idea for this project when I had to go through my old work to send something to an art show, and found myself wading through volumes and volumes of my old comic diaries, obsessively kept over the years.

MY GOD, WHAT A COLOSSAL WASTE OF TALENT! WHAT WILL COME OF ALL THIS!? I DON'T EVEN SEEM TO IMPROVE MUCH, I'M JUST BETTER SOMETIMES AND WORSE OTHER TIMES.

Of course it's mostly unfinished, unpublishable, insignificant stuff.

WHY DID I SPEND SO MUCH ENERGY ON THAT GUY ANYWAY?

IT ALL SEEMED SO MONUMENTAL AT THE TIME.

The reasons I started this thing were:

- I do a diary comic every day anyway.
- Need a sense of accomplishment.
- Need attention.
- Need "internet presence."
- Need creative challenge.
- Secretly hoping somehow it could lead to making $$$.
- Nothing seems to ever work out for me so I might as well do exactly what I want to do, which is this.

The problem is, at the time I decided to start this thing I was having a good day.

THAT DAY:

THIS IS EASY AND FUN! I COULD DO THIS EVERY DAY! I MUST SHARE IT WITH THE WORLD!

MOST DAYS:

THIS IS HARD AND HUMILIATING! I MUST CONCEAL THIS PATHETIC ATTEMPT AT "SELF EXPRESSION" FROM THE WORLD!

# Wednesday, July sixth

I went to the post office to mail some stuff.

EXCUSE ME, ARE YOU IN LINE?

I'VE BEEN THROUGH THAT FUCKIN' LINE THREE TIMES. I'D SUGGEST YOU COME BACK ANOTHER DAY.

OH, SHIT. I WILL.

WHY DID WE INTRODUCE INTIMATE BODILY FUNCTIONS INTO THAT BRIEF CONVERSATION BETWEEN STRANGERS?

I went back early the next morning. I decided I needed more tape on one of my packages so I used some of the "express mail" tape, cutting it with my keys.

I AM DOING A STUPID THING RIGHT NOW AND I KNOW IT AND I'M NOT EVEN STOPPING MYSELF.

WILL SOMEONE PLEASE STOP ME?

Suddenly I couldn't remember if I needed to send the package U.P.S. or U.S.P.S.

U.P.S. IS A WHOLE DIFFERENT COMPANY. WHICH IS IT?

WELL, I HAVE THIS ACCOUNT NUMBER I'M SUPPOSED TO USE.

THE FIRST THING YOU'RE GOING TO HAVE TO DO IS TAKE THAT EXPRESS MAIL TAPE OFF.

But in fact the first thing I needed to do was go home and figure out if I needed to send it U.P.S. or U.S.P.S.

I forgot my keys.

Luckily the super had an extra pair for just such an occasion.

AGAIN!? WE SHOULD HIDE A SET IN THE TREE OUT FRONT FOR YOU.

OR MAYBE I SHOULD JUST LIVE IN THE TREE.

I biked back to the post office.

EXCUSE ME, YOU CAN'T BRING YOUR BIKE IN HERE!

I JUST FORGOT MY KEYS!

WHAT DO THEY LOOK LIKE?

KEYS!

WHAT'S ON THEM?

KEYS. A BIKE KEY.

SHE'S GOT SOME KEYS OVER THERE.

YES! THOSE ARE MINE!

I WILL GIVE YOU YOUR KEYS WHEN YOU TAKE YOUR BIKE OUT OF THE BUILDING.

UNITED STATES POSTAL SERVICE

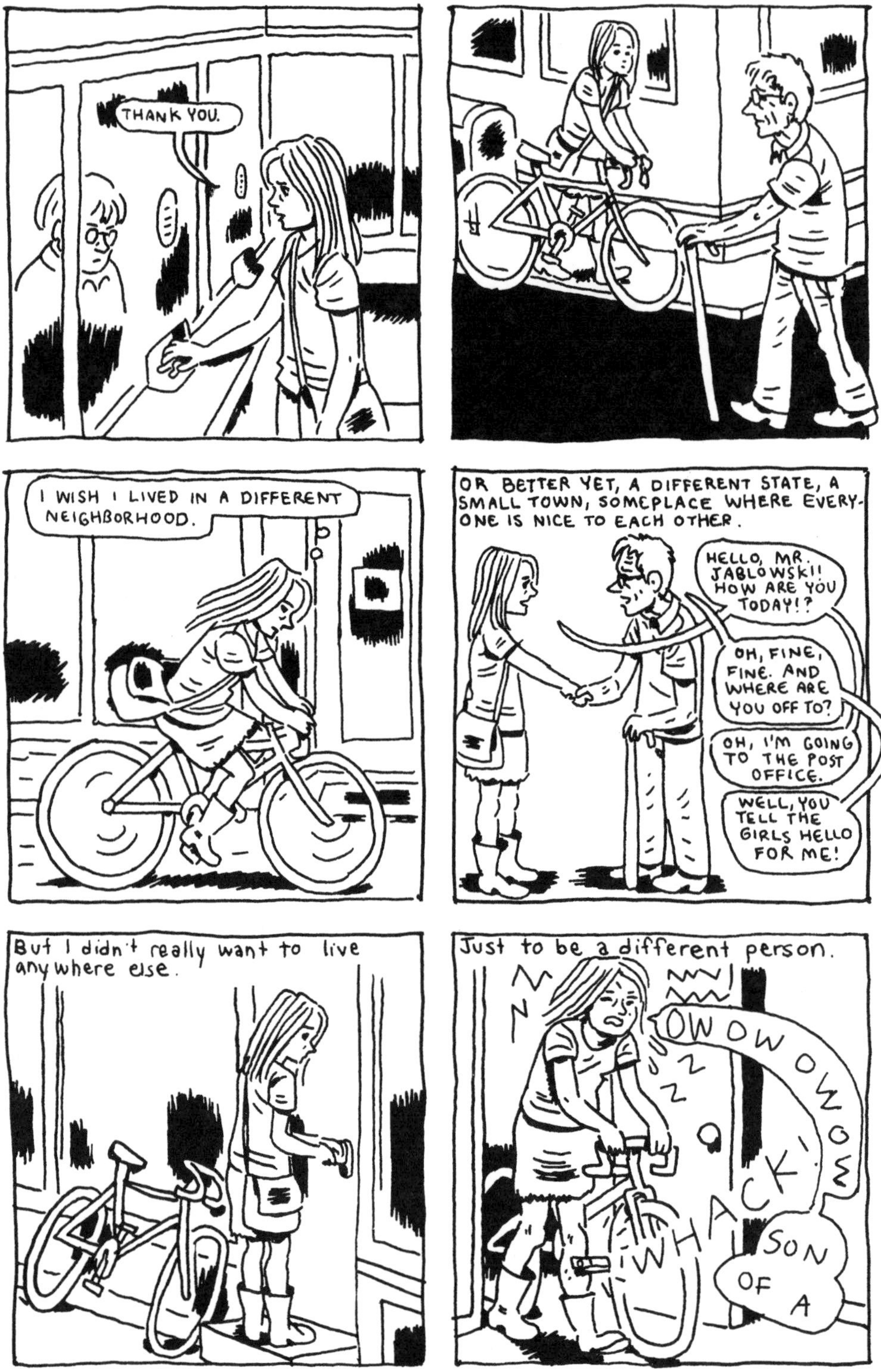

THANK YOU.
I WISH I LIVED IN A DIFFERENT NEIGHBORHOOD.
OR BETTER YET, A DIFFERENT STATE, A SMALL TOWN, SOMEPLACE WHERE EVERYONE IS NICE TO EACH OTHER.
HELLO, MR. JABLOWSKI! HOW ARE YOU TODAY!?
OH, FINE, FINE. AND WHERE ARE YOU OFF TO?
OH, I'M GOING TO THE POST OFFICE.
WELL, YOU TELL THE GIRLS HELLO FOR ME!
But I didn't really want to live anywhere else.
Just to be a different person.
OWOWOWOWOW
WHACK
SON OF A

Saturday, July ninth

An elderly gentleman came to repair something in the bathroom.

He didn't speak English.

He worked himself into a rage when he couldn't make me understand that he wanted to build me some cabinets.

# Sunday, July tenth

Each time I walk to yoga class I do this exercise where I attempt to untangle all of my thoughts.

I WONDER WHAT HE'S DOING. IS HE MAD AT ME? AM I MAD AT HIM?

WAIT, WHY DID I SUDDENLY START THINKING ABOUT CHAD?

OH! IT'S BECAUSE ONCE I WAS TALKING WITH HIM FOR A LONG TIME AND STARING AT THAT SAME VAN. NOW THAT VAN WILL ALWAYS REMIND ME OF CHAD.

I sometimes get bursts of cruel, un-justified, irrational anger.

YOU GOTTA BE A WALKING, I MEAN ROLLING REPROACH TO US ALL, DON'T YOU.

VIET NAM VET

And of love.

I LOVE THIS OLD LADY SO MUCH.

IS IT JUST BECAUSE SHE IS WEARING ORANGE LIPSTICK LIKE MY DEAR OLD ENGLISH GRANDMOTHER?

Other times I'll see something that will jar me out of my head. Like this man lumbering down Berry street. Instead of falling forward from one foot to the next like most of us, he was shifting his weight back and forth from side to side, scuttling along like a top-heavy crab.

IS THIS THE PROPER WAY TO WALK?

# Monday, July eleventh

What a nice day it was! first I went to Eight Avenue & 34th street and had a pleasant Post Office experience.

NEXT IN LINE, PLEASE PROCEED TO ASSOCIATE NUMBER TEN.

Then to the U.P.S. place on Eighth Avenue & 27th (the package was U.P.S.)

WE'LL TAKE CARE OF THIS FOR YOU.

Then to the Gagosian Gallery on 21st street to see picasso's Marie-Thérèse paintings.

Then down to Nicolas Robinson gallery on 20th street to see Jason Polan's Artist-in-residence show where Jason was hanging out with Victor Kerlow and filling the walls with his famous New York drawings.

WHAT ARE THE BIG DARK SPOTS ABOUT?

I JUST LIKE THE WAY THEY LOOK.

Next, me, Jason and Victor continued down Eighth Avenue to another art show in Tribecca.

I WENT TO THIS ICE CREAM SHOP ON THE HIGHLINE WHERE THEY HAVE ICE CREAM SANDWICHES THE SIZE OF YOUR HEAD AND IF YOU EAT THE WHOLE THING IT'S FREE, SO I ATE IT ALL AND GOT TOTALLY SICK BUT NOW MY ICE CREAM TOLERANCE THRESHOLD HAS GONE WAY UP.

We saw many sights on our way downtown including:
The Façade that was filmed in the opening credits of The Cosby Show.

THAT ONE THERE.

An old Keith Haring mural by the public pool on seventh Avenue.

WNYC BUILDING

OMIGOD DO YOU THINK BRIAN LEHRER'S IN THERE?

HAVE YOU SEEN HIM? HE LOOKS LIKE SOME GUY WHO SITS AROUND AND READS LORD OF THE RINGS ALL DAY.

A MAGAZINE IN A SHOP THAT HAD VICTOR'S DRAWINGS IN IT.

SHOULD I BUY IT? NAH. I'LL GET A FREE ONE.

SNIP
SNIP

SEXY BABE

The Barber-shop where Jason used to go to that had porno magazines

WHAT DID THEY EXPECT US TO DO WITH THEM?

When we arrived at the show, we were all sweaty and exhausted.

WELL, WE'VE GOTTA GO NOW.

Then I met up with other friends and we went on to do a bunch more things, but I could not stop thinking about that head-sized ice cream sandwich.

HEY YOU GUYS LET'S GET SOME ICE CREAM.

# Tuesday, July Twelfth

Got a haircut for Lizz's & my event this Thursday, because I don't want to look like a hippy mom anymore.

CAN YOU MAKE ME LOOK ...

MORE LIKE YOU?

Because I had no time for the itchy, nervous, empty, despairing, angry, directionless feeling I get pretty much every afternoon, I went jogging to try to get rid of it.

had a celebratory dinner with Sadie, who'd just gotten her commercial pilot's license, an accomplishment she's been working towards for like years.

WHY DO I KEEP FILLING UP ON BREAD? BECAUSE IT'S FREE?! WHEN WILL I GROW OUT OF THAT MINDSET?

MAYBE YOU COULD JUST THINK OF THE BREAD AS YOUR DINNER AND DINNER AS YOUR DESSERT.

When I got home I realized I'd lost my keys again. Not exactly lost, I'd detached them from the rest of my keys so they wouldn't jangle around in my pocket while I jogged.

But I was too embarrassed to tell that to the super again.

HI! YOU GOING UP-STAIRS?

NAH, I WAS JUST LEAVING.

So I went to Tony's to wait until my roommate came home. Tony gave me a bowl of ice cream and a glass of prosecco and told me about Jaume Plensa's Echo sculpture in Madison Square Park.

IT'S THIS BIG WEIRD *HEAD*, ONLY STRETCHED OUT IN THIS SORT OF CINEMA-SCOPIC COMPUTERESE.

IT DOESN'T MAKE SENSE TO SEE IT LIKE THIS.

IT'S LIKE THE MOST AMAZING SERENE STRANGE THING.

YOU WALK UP TO IT AND YOU'RE LIKE, WOW.

## Wednesday, July thirteenth

Tony came by to help move some books to Desert Island.

WHY DON'T YOU MAKE THIS SO IT DOESN'T LOCK AUTOMATICALLY? YOU'LL HAVE TO LOCK IT ON YOUR WAY OUT SO YOU'LL NEVER FORGET YOUR KEYS!

BUT THEN I'LL FORGET TO LOCK IT. I'D RATHER LOCK MYSELF OUT THAN LEAVE THE DOOR UNLOCKED.

AFTER ALL, I HAVE BACK UP! THERE'S MY ROOMMATE, AND MY SUPER, AND NOW YOU—

AND ANOTHER THING! WHEN THE PLUMBER ASKS IF YOU HAVE A BOYFRIEND, YOU SAY YES!

WHY DO YOU HAVE TO LECTURE ME SO MUCH? MAYBE I WANTED TO BE HIT ON.

I'M NOT LECTURING! I'M TELLING YOU THAT SOMETIMES IT IS OKAY TO LIE, ESPECIALLY WHEN IT COMES TO YOUR PERSONAL SAFETY.

HAS THERE EVER BEEN A TIME WHEN YOU'VE SUCCEEDED IN GETTING ME TO DO SOMETHING BY LECTURING OR NAGGING ME ABOUT IT?

WELL, THERE WAS THAT TIME YOU NAGGED ME TO STOP PAYING MY BILLS BY CHECK AND START PAYING ONLINE.

THAT'S ONLY COMMON SENSE!

HI GABE!

HEY GUYS!

SO WE'VE GOT TWENTY WHEN I'M OLDS, THREE LUCKIES, TWO CECIL & JORDANS AND TEN POSTERS.

GOT IT.

I MEAN WHY WOULD ANYONE WANT TO SPEND ALL THAT TIME AND MONEY GOING TO THE POST OFFICE AND BUYING STAMPS AND ORDERING CHECKS AND BUYING ENVELOPES AND WRITING IT ALL OUT AND GOING TO THE MAILBOX WHEN YOU CAN GO ONLINE AND—

WILL YOU STOP!? I'VE ALREADY ADMITTED YOU WERE RIGHT AND SWITCHED TO ONLINE!

OH YEAH! I WON THAT ONE.

Thursday, July fourteenth

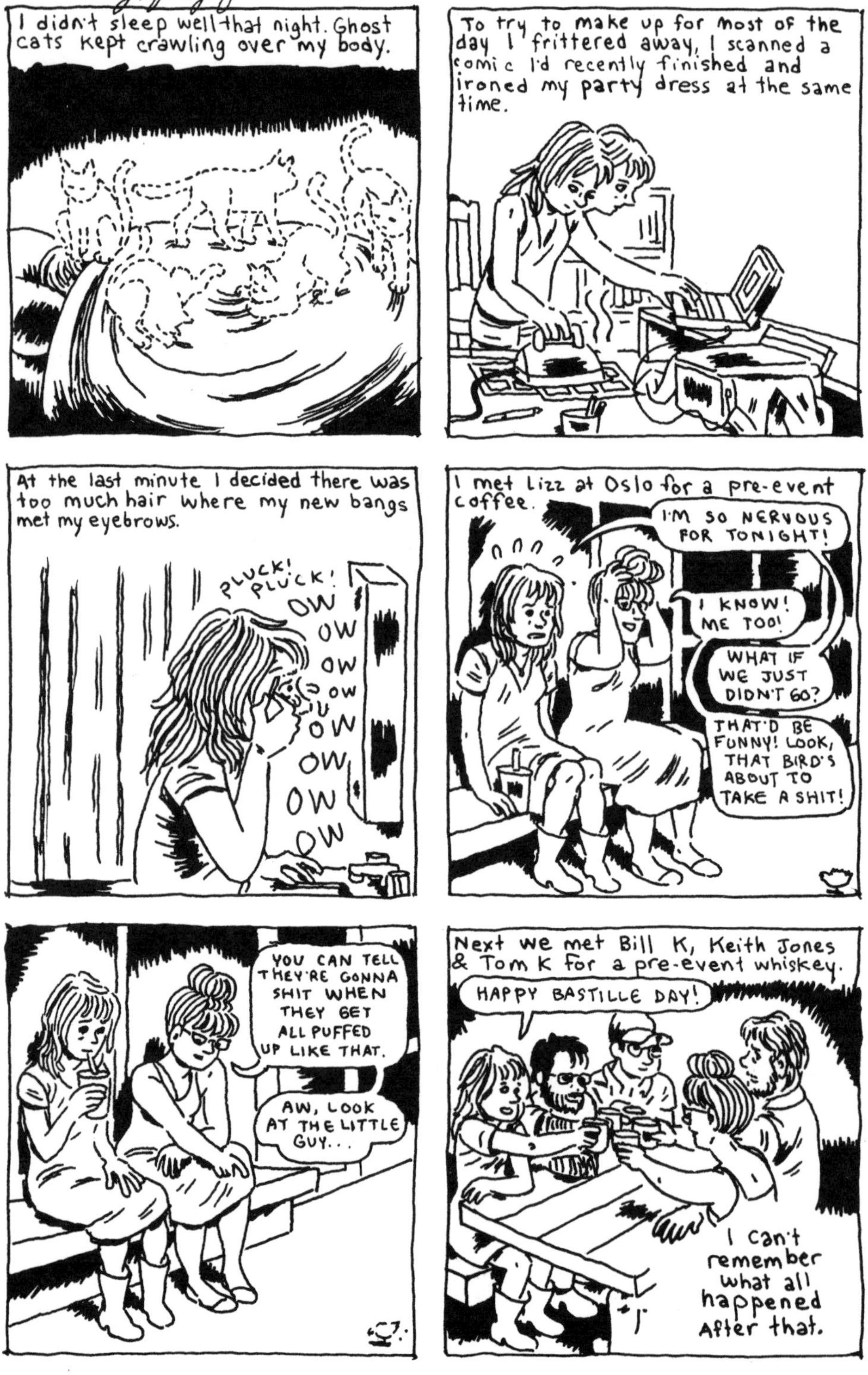
I didn't sleep well that night. Ghost cats kept crawling over my body.
To try to make up for most of the day I frittered away, I scanned a comic I'd recently finished and ironed my party dress at the same time.
At the last minute I decided there was too much hair where my new bangs met my eyebrows.
PLUCK! PLUCK!
OW OW OW OW OW OW OW OW
I met Lizz at Oslo for a pre-event coffee.
I'M SO NERVOUS FOR TONIGHT!
I KNOW! ME TOO!
WHAT IF WE JUST DIDN'T GO?
THAT'D BE FUNNY! LOOK, THAT BIRD'S ABOUT TO TAKE A SHIT!
YOU CAN TELL THEY'RE GONNA SHIT WHEN THEY GET ALL PUFFED UP LIKE THAT.
AW, LOOK AT THE LITTLE GUY...
Next we met Bill K, Keith Jones & Tom K for a pre-event whiskey.
HAPPY BASTILLE DAY!
I can't remember what all happened After that.

# Friday, July fifteenth

As I woke up my old fan was rattling in such a way that made it sound like it was raining so hard outside the streets were flooding.

I had to go to the window to check. It was dry and sunny just like any other July morning.

I was so tired, all I could do was sit around reading comics all day.

CRIME

Went with Tom k to Desert Island to see about how many comics we sold. I read Cowboy Henk comics while the guys nerded out about music.

I WAS REALLY INTO ETHNOGRAPHIC FUNK AT THE TIME AND HE WAS ALL, WHAT IS THIS ETHNOGRAPHIC FUNK YOU'RE PLAYING.

HA HA EW! HE CUTS A HOLE IN HIS CHEEK AND THEN HE TRIES TO TONGUE-KISS HIS GRANDMOTHER THROUGH THE SIDE OF HIS FACE!

I hurried home to read more comics and lay around. When I get so tired I can't fight off the feeling of hopelessness, despair and contradiction that seem to always follow me.

I AM SO LONELY...

AND YET I CAN'T STAND THE COMPANY OF ANYONE...

That is when the place fills up with ghost cats.

MEOW
ARG! GET OUT OF HERE!
MEOW
MEOW
MEOW
MEOW
MEOW
MEOW

# Saturday, July sixteenth

Karen got me a job in Midtown, disconnecting computers and reconnecting them in another building.

WATCH OUT, YOU'RE TOTALLY GONNA GET HIT ON BY THE MOVERS!

OH, GOOD, I'VE BEEN FEELING FRUMPY LATELY.

THANKS FOR THE CLIFF BAR! I FEEL KINDA BAD TAKING YOUR FOOD!

DON'T WORRY, I CAN ALWAYS GET ANOTHER ONE ON OUR LUNCH BREAK!

OH, WE DON'T GET A LUNCH BREAK.

WAIT, WHAT? NO FOOD FOR EIGHT HOURS?

WELL, SOMETIMES THERE'LL BE A BAGEL PLATTER SITTING AROUND.

CAN WE AT LEAST STOP AT A STORE NOW AND GRAB A SNACK?

NOT ALLOWED! WE'RE ON THE CLOCK!

HEY, I'M GONNA STOP IN DAT DUANE READE AND GET A RED BULL!

QUICK! LET'S FOLLOW HIM!

LOOK, THE MEN DON'T EVEN QUESTION IF THEY'RE ALLOWED!

I KNOW, WE'RE LIKE TWO BABY DUCKS FOLLOWING THE MAMA DUCK.

WE GOTTA HURRY! IF WE LOSE THE OTHERS WE'RE SCREWED! I DON'T KNOW WHERE WE'RE GOING! I'M GETTING THESE!

FIBER BAR

KUDOS

I'LL GET THESE!

WE'RE GONNA BE FARTING ALL DAY!

WE WILL BE FUELED BY FART POWER!

SO IT'S SIMPLE, ALL YOU GOTTA DO IS TAKE THE VGI CABLE AND UNPLUG IT FROM THE CPU BUT WHATEVER YOU DO DON'T TAKE THE LAN CABLE AND FILL OUT DIS FORM TO CORRESPOND WITH THE COLOR COORDINATES AND DON'T FORGET TO PUT IN YOUR CODE NUMBER WHICH IN DIS CASE IS A17 BUT CHECK AND WRITE DOWN IF IT'S A CPU OR A UPC AND YOU KEEP DIS FORM AND PUT DIS FORM IN A BAG WITH EVERYTHING ELSE AND DAT'S DAT, YOU'RE DONE.

KAREN! I HAVE NO IDEA WHAT TO DO! WHAT'S A VGI CABLE?! WHAT'S A CPU? WHAT'S A LAN CABLE?!

AW, IT'S EASY! JUST PUT EVERYTHING IN A BAG AND WRITE IT DOWN!

Soon I figured it out, and it was easy and fun, packing everything up and writing it down.

It was nice to be way up there watching all the people and cars moving around like tiny parts of a huge machine.

And all those cubicles! What do they **DO** in those cubicles all day?

I imagine someone feeling so trapped, taking every opportunity to escape into cyberspace.

After exhausting herself on the internet, I imagine an attempt to reach out to the other inmates.

But who can blame her here?

The second half of the shift, setting up computer stations in big glass-walled offices, was harder.

THERE'S NO CPU DOWN HERE!

PLUG EVERYTHING IN THAT YOU CAN FOR NOW.

BUT EVERY THING PLUGS INTO THE CPU!

In some offices there were tiny rooms with no apparent use overlooking the city.

I WONDER IF THIS WAS BUILT JUST FOR THE EXECUTIVES SO THEY WON'T GO CRAZY FROM FEELING LIKE THEY LIVE IN A FISH BOWL.

I FARTED.

GET ME OUT OF HERE!

FROM NOW ON I'M DEEMING THIS THE FART CAVE!

We got out at 2:30 A.M, and Karen had to work at 8:00 the next morning.

I'M WORRIED THE L TRAIN IS GONNA BE ALL WEIRD TONIGHT.

TAKE THE E WITH ME! YOU CAN TRANSFER TO COURT SQUARE AND IT'LL TAKE YOU RIGHT THERE. IT'LL BE EASY.

We spaced out, got on the wrong train and ended up in the Bronx.

SHOULD WE GO BACK TO THE L? SHOULD WE GET A CAB?

HOW DID WE LET THIS HAPPEN?

GABRIELLE, YOU SAID THIS WOULD BE EASY!

WELL... YOU SAID I'D GET HIT ON!

NOT ONE GUY SPOKE TO ME!

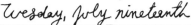

I borrowed Tony's computer again for my intern Daryl to use.

SORRY. I PROMISE I'LL HAVE MY OWN PHOTOSHOP WORKING AGAIN NEXT WEEK.

WHY DON'T YOU JUST PUT EVERYTHING ON YOUR EXTERNAL DRIVE AND WIPE THE WHOLE THING CLEAN?

MY EXTERNAL DRIVE IS FULL. BY THE WAY, DID YOU THROW OUT THOSE FILES I LEFT ON YOUR DESKTOP?

YEAH, I NEEDED TO MAKE SPACE FOR MY VIDEOS. DID YOU NEED THEM?

OH NO! I JUST REALIZED I DIDN'T BACK THEM UP! THAT WAS ALL THE COLORING WORK THAT DARYL DID!

I DIDN'T KNOW. I CONSIDERED CALLING AND ASKING BUT I THOUGHT, WHY WOULD SHE LEAVE STUFF ON MY DESKTOP WITHOUT BACKING IT UP?

I FORGOT! I'VE BEEN SO BUSY I JUST FORGOT! HOW AM I GOING TO TELL HER I JUST THREW OUT TWO DAYS OF HER WORK!?

DON'T TELL HER! JUST MOVE ON TO THE NEXT THING!

SHE'LL WANT TO KNOW! SHE'LL ASK WHAT HAPPENED TO IT!

TELL HER YOU WEREN'T HAPPY WITH WHAT SHE'S DONE AND SHE'S GOTTA REDO IT. IT WILL BE BETTER THE NEXT TIME!

NOT EVERYTHING HAPPENS FOR THE BEST! SOMETIMES THINGS HAPPEN FOR THE WORST!

SO THIS IS THE WORST THING THAT COULD HAPPEN?

NO, NOT THE WORST. BUT REALLY, REALLY BAD!

SO WHAT CAN WE LEARN FROM THIS?

NOTHING! BECAUSE I'VE DONE STUPID SHIT LIKE THIS BEFORE AND I WILL AGAIN BECAUSE I AM HOPELESS AND INCOMPETENT!

JUST MOVE ON TO THE NEXT PAGE!

WHAT'S THE POINT.

THE IMPORTANT THING IS TO MOVE FORWARD.

YOU'VE GOT TO MOVE FORWARD!

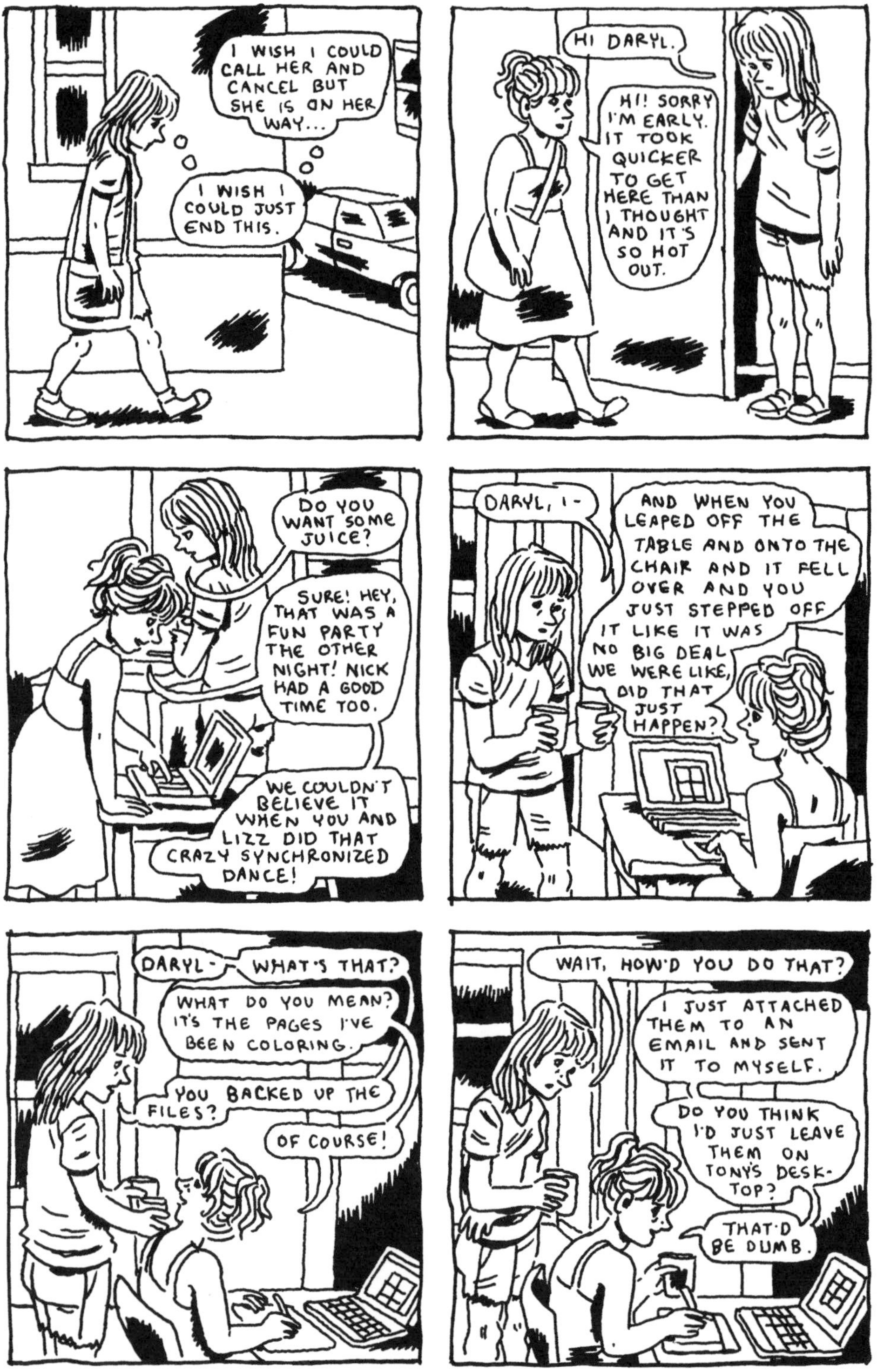
I WISH I COULD CALL HER AND CANCEL BUT SHE IS ON HER WAY...
I WISH I COULD JUST END THIS.
HI DARYL.
HI! SORRY I'M EARLY. IT TOOK QUICKER TO GET HERE THAN I THOUGHT AND IT'S SO HOT OUT.
DO YOU WANT SOME JUICE?
SURE! HEY, THAT WAS A FUN PARTY THE OTHER NIGHT! NICK HAD A GOOD TIME TOO.
WE COULDN'T BELIEVE IT WHEN YOU AND LIZZ DID THAT CRAZY SYNCHRONIZED DANCE!
DARYL, I-
AND WHEN YOU LEAPED OFF THE TABLE AND ONTO THE CHAIR AND IT FELL OVER AND YOU JUST STEPPED OFF IT LIKE IT WAS NO BIG DEAL WE WERE LIKE, DID THAT JUST HAPPEN?
DARYL-
WHAT'S THAT?
WHAT DO YOU MEAN? IT'S THE PAGES I'VE BEEN COLORING.
YOU BACKED UP THE FILES?
OF COURSE!
WAIT, HOW'D YOU DO THAT?
I JUST ATTACHED THEM TO AN EMAIL AND SENT IT TO MYSELF.
DO YOU THINK I'D JUST LEAVE THEM ON TONY'S DESK-TOP?
THAT'D BE DUMB.

# Thursday, July twenty-first

When I walk down the street the Kooks & the wingnuts glare at me accusingly. They know I am just barely able to pass.

TRAITOR

And what about this drunk Polish guy in the Darth Vader mask scaring people at two on a Sunday afternoon? He accomplished more that morning than I had all weekend.

RAWWR!

PEACE MY BROTHER!

And then there's Tessie. All day and night she moves her belongings, piece by piece, up and down Manhattan Avenue, back and forth, in 100 or 10 degree weather.

Sometimes she sings to herself, other times she's too weary.

Every time I see her my heart dislocates all over again.

WHY WON'T SOMEONE INTERVENE? CAN'T SOMEBODY DO SOMETHING?!?

Once I saw this Hasidic Jewish guy, completely undone, ranting and raving what must've been gibberish in Yiddish, barreling in my direction.

UH OH, LOOKS LIKE I'M WITHIN PUNCHING DISTANCE!

But.

OH.

blue tooth

## Friday, July twenty-second

Oh, boy, is it hot enough for you? It sure is hot! It's really hot! I'll tell you. It's a hot one.

Anyway. I have ten days left of this arbitrary, self-imposed month of daily comics regime and it is starting to wear on me.

OMIGOD MY FILES ARE LOST FOREVER!

AH, JEEZ, I'M GONNA HAVE TO DO A COMIC ABOUT THIS.

It's not so easy, I can't just crank these things out. I have to try to reveal enough to create some sort of emotional impact but not so much that anyone feels compromised. And the most interesting stories are the ones I can never tell.

BEFORE I TELL YOU THIS YOU HAVE TO PROMISE YOU WON'T DO A COMIC ABOUT IT.

WHAT IF I CHANGED YOUR IDENTITY?

To get something that works I have to set up the best conditions, which requires a certain diligence that pretty much takes over my whole life.

And then all I can do is wait and hope for the lightning of inspiration to strike.

But why am I even doing this? Why not simply write fiction? Why do I have to put my own feeble life into these panels? Is it a natural reaction in todays alienated society or is it a disorder?

HEY EVERY ONE!!!

I EXIST

Saturday, July twenty-third

I wish somebody would drive up in front of my apartment and honk twice.

BE RIGHT DOWN!

and take me away from the city as I watch buildings gradually give way to trees.

We'd arrive at a big old house with the sound of children shouting coming from somewhere.

WELCOME!

I'd put my stuff down in my room whose window would overlook the backyard which would be an endless wilderness.

I'd quickly change and run barefoot to join the children down at the lake.

EEEEEE!!

GABRIELLE!

I'd stay on after everyone had left to look after the place. I'd read and work on my novel. I'd stop updating my blog because all I'd have to say in it would be things like, "It snowed today."

I'm having trouble finishing up my Kramers comic. I've spent such a long time on it, I want it to be perfect.

LET ME SHOW IT TO A FEW PEOPLE BEFORE I DECLARE IT FINISHED.

WHO ARE YOU GONNA SHOW IT TO? I'VE READ YOUR BLOG, YOU HANG OUT WITH A BUNCH OF LUNATICS!

Anyway, Daryl came over to help me color, and Michel kept bothering me about having dinner.

I CAN'T TODAY. HOW ABOUT TUESDAY?

NO, TODAY.

WHY CAN'T YOU EVER MAKE A PLAN?

YES, IN TEN MINUTES.

When we finished we went to return the computer we borrowed from Tony.

COME ON! I WILL TAKE YOU OUT FOR SUSHI!

ONLY IF YOU TAKE MY INTERN AND TONY OUT FOR SUSHI TOO.

OKAY, FINE.

So Michel took us all out for a big sushi boat.

I WANT TO TAKE THIS THING AND SAIL IT DOWN THE EAST RIVER!

DID YOU KNOW SCHEDULES WERE FIRST INVENTED ON THE PORTS OF THE EAST RIVER? BEFORE THAT SHIPS WOULD SHOW UP WHENEVER AND CAUSE ALL THIS CHAOS.

W-WHAT, WAIT, WHAT DO YOU KNOW ABOUT SCHEDULES?

DID YOU JUST STUTTER?! YOU KNOW I WAS JUST WATCHING THIS DOCUMENTARY ABOUT BILL WITHERS, HE HAD A STUTTER. YOU KNOW HOW HE GOT OVER IT? BEFORE EACH INTERACTION HE'D SAY TO HIMSELF: "I FORGIVE THIS PERSON IN ADVANCE FOR THE JUDGEMENT THEY'LL BESTOW ON ME!"

OKAY MICHEL, I FORGIVE YOU FOR ALL THE MEAN THINGS YOU'LL SAY TO ME TONIGHT.

YEAH, RIGHT! YOU'LL CARRY A GRUDGE AGAINST ME FOREVER.

I finally finished coloring my Kramers' Ergot comic. It's only five pages, but it's a dense little story.

LET ME KNOW IF SOMETHING DOESN'T MAKE SENSE OR IF YOU SEE A MISTAKE.

THE GUY'S HAIR COLOR IS DIFFERENT IN PANELS FIVE AND SIX.

THAT'S BECAUSE IT'S TEN YEARS LATER, HE'S GONE GRAY.

OH, I SEE.

SO YOU'RE NOT GOING TO INCLUDE THE EPILOGUE YOU HAD IN THE EARLIER DRAFT?

NAH. I DECIDED IT'S BETTER TO LET THE READER IMAGINE WHAT BECAME OF HER.

WHAT ABOUT IN TRUE GRIT? WE SEE HOW THE GIRL TURNED OUT IN THAT MOVIE.

THAT'S TRUE! THAT WORKED. I GUESS THAT EPILOGUE WAS TRUE TO THE STORY AND WELL WRITTEN, AND THERE WAS SOMETHING FALSE AND FORCED ABOUT MINE.

I DON'T KNOW. I DIDN'T LIKE KNOWING WHAT HAPPENED.

For the past month the one thought in my head has been, "finish this comic." Now it was: "Celebrate!"

We went to Karen, Joan & Robyn's yet-to-be-named studio where Jon Lewis was celebrating his birthday, by, funnily enough, watching True Grit.

I FINISHED COLORING MY KRAMERS COMIC!

JESSE REKLAW

I STILL HAVE TO COLOR MY SLOW WAVE COMIC. IT'S DUE TOMORROW.

YOU GOTTA GET ON THAT!

I couldn't focus on the film because Jesse was coloring in front of me.

WHY IS EVERYBODY SPEAKING IN COMPLETE SENTENCES IN THIS FILM?

WHEN'S HE GONNA FILL IN THAT WHITE TRIANGLE!?

WHAT COLOR WILL HE USE?!!

IS HIS PROCESS BETTER THAN MINE?

ARG! FILL IN THE TRIANGLE ALREADY!

# Tuesday, July twenty sixth

Met Lauren Weinstein in Madison Square Park to see Echo.

IF YOU SEE HER AT DIFFERENT TIMES OF THE DAY SHE TAKES ON DIFFERENT QUALITIES.

In the mornings it's closed off here and there's something mystical about her.

In the afternoons the sunbathers come out and she becomes this monument to beauty.

In the evening it becomes mommy hour.

SHE DEFINITELY HAS AN EFFECT ON PEOPLE.

IT'S LIKE SHE'S IN THIS MOMENT OF EXHALATION.

I THINK SHE'S THE MOST BEAUTIFUL LADY EVER.

Of course if you saw the rest of her it'd be scary.

## Wednesday, July twenty-seventh

Hi! Sorry for no comic today. I'm on vacation! Here's some snapshots of my amazing trip! Don't be jealous! Here I am, firesurfing! I know! Me! Right?

Boy, that was hot! To cool off I swung from one side of a giant waterfall to the other by a rope attached to... wait, I don't even know what it was attached to! Oh well! It was refreshing!

After that I was so hungry I ate an entire active volcano! I still have heartburn, ha ha! See me waving there? Good times.

I was pretty tired out but I always wanted to try catbackriding and how many chances am I gonna get?

Then there was this little mishap!

EEK!

WOOF!! WOOF! WOOF WOOF WOOF WOOF!

So.... yeah, I'm still on vacation. I guess I'm dogbackriding now. Please send help! I want to come home.

# Thursday, July twenty eighth

Just Movie Night with Tony.

THE SMELL OF THAT ORANGE, IT REMINDS ME OF SOMETHING...

ANOTHER TIME YOU HAD AN ORANGE?

NO, IT REMINDS ME OF A TIME WHEN SMELLING AN ORANGE MEANT SOMETHING TO ME.

POP!! POP! POP!

LIKE...WHEN A WOMAN WALKS PAST YOU AND THE SMELL OF HER PERFUME TRANSFORMS YOUR WHOLE BEING.

WHEN I REALLY FELT THE THINGS I DID. LIKE DRINKING A BEER. NOW I JUST DO IT OUT OF HABIT. THERE'S NO REAL PLEASURE IN IT.

BUT YOU MUST ENJOY IT A LITTLE?

I REMEMBER THE FIRST TIME I DRANK BEER. IT WAS SO DIFFERENT FROM THIS. I WAS RIDING ON A BIKE WITH THIS CUBAN BOY AND WE TURNED THE CORNER AND SAW THE LIGHTS OF THE CARNIVAL...

MUNCH

SORRY BUT ALL I HAVE IS 'LOVE STORY.' I HOPE IT'S NOT AWFUL.

CARNIVAL LIGHTS ALWAYS CAUSE EXCITEMENT IN YOUNG PEOPLE.

THEN THIS CAR CAME AROUND THE CORNER AND WE CRASHED INTO THE DITCH AND IT WAS PAINFUL AND SCARY BUT SO EXHILARATING AND I THOUGHT: 'I AM DRUNK!'

I GUESS THE DIFFERENCE IS INNOCENCE.

BUT I THINK PEOPLE ROMANTICIZE INNOCENCE.

IT'S TRUE! I JUST REMEMBER FEELING FEAR PRETTY MUCH ALL THE TIME.

FOR ME IT WAS SHAME.

YES! SHAME AND FEAR AND HOPE AND DISAPPOINTMENT.

WHY WON'T THIS DVD WORK!?

THAT MUST BE WHY PEOPLE HAVE CHILDREN, TO TRY TO BRING THAT INNOCENCE BACK.

I STILL FEEL FEAR AND SHAME AND HOPE AND DISAPPOINTMENT ALL THE TIME.

SORRY, WE CAN'T WATCH THIS MOVIE. IT'S THE WRONG COUNTRY CODE.

# Friday, July twenty-ninth

Last night on my way home, worried about having no material for today's comic, I began to eavesdrop on the people ahead of me, in which a guy was talking about foreskins, yeast infections and chronic rectal bleeding.

When he saw what I was doing he slowed down, spoke louder and repeated himself to make sure I got everything.

When they stopped at a bar I was invited to join.

He also talked about doing drugs, face punching, buttfucking, casual sex and venereal diseases.

WHAT HAPPENED TO YOUR ARM?

HE BROKE IT PUNCHING HIM.

WHY DID YOU PUNCH HIM?

IT'S NOT MY FAULT! HE PROVOKED ME!

OH. FAIR ENOUGH.

# Saturday, July thirtieth

Waiting for Sadie to have fancy cocktails.

AND ORDER, OR WE'LL BE LATE FOR THE SHOW.

WE SHOULD GO IN

WE'LL BE FINE, SHE'LL GET HERE

I FEEL CRAPPY. I SHOULD BE EATING KALE ALL THE TIME OR SOMETHING.

I'VE BEEN EATING KALE ALL THE TIME AND I STILL FEEL CRAPPY! REMEMBER THAT BIOSPHERE EXPERIMENT IN THE NINETIES?

NO.

They couldn't grow enough food and they were half starved all the time. The medic was the guy who believed if you cut your caloric intake way down and mostly ate vegetables you'd live much longer. But everyone was miserable and fighting and stealing and going crazy.

THIS IS AN IDEAL DIET WE'RE ON!

That makes me think of this story I read about these two guys stuck in a cabin in the klondike all winter who went crazy. They kept going outside and losing fingers and toes and cheeks and noses. They ended up killing each other over a cup of sugar.

BUT NOT EVERYONE WOULD REACT THAT WAY. SHACKLETON AND HIS MEN SURVIVED FOR MONTHS ALL HUDDLED IN A LITTLE TENT WITH BARELY ANYTHING TO EAT AND THEY HELD IT TOGETHER

YOU HAVEN'T STARTED YET? WE'RE GOING TO BE LATE FOR THE SHOW!

WE WERE WAITING FOR YOU!

I THOUGHT YOU'D START WITHOUT ME!

WE SHOULD JUST GO. ALENE WILL BE WAITING FOR US.

BUT THIS GROUPON EXPIRES TOMORROW!

LET'S JUST GO IN FOR TWENTY MINUTES!

But the place was so enchanting we lost all sense of time.

THIS IS SUCH A DATE PLACE! BUT I'M GLAD I'M WITH YOU GUYS AND NOT ON A DATE. IT'D BE TOO MUCH.

I KNOW, YOU WOULDN'T BE ABLE TO KEEP A STRAIGHT FACE.

THAT'D BE FUNNY IF WE WERE ON A THREESOME-DATE FROM SOME WEIRD MÉNAGE À TROIS VERSION OF OKCUPID.

# Sunday, July thirty-first

Tony says he doesn't want to see me do any more comics about me doing comics. Also he doesn't want me to use the word "just" anymore. But it's the end of my 31-day comic experiment and I'm just about out of everything. I'm even down to the last few drops of ink.

He also doesn't want to see me complain anymore, but boy, this has been hard! It feels like I've distorted myself beyond recognition, and it will take some time to return to my original form, if that's even possible.

The first couple weeks weren't so bad, but then things started closing in on me; I was running out of material, things began to fall apart.

I kept having to switch up my routine. Like at first exercising every day helped, then stopping exercising every day worked, then stopping stopped working, and then I started following strangers into bars.

Am I done yet? What? Still two more panels? Come on! I've got shit to do!

In conclusion, comics are hard! And life is too! But from now on everything is going to be a breeze! Just like I thought this project would be! Un oh! It looks like I'm running out of

ARG!!

I went with Richard to an Oscar party. It was all the way outside of New York, and Richard rented a Zipcar.

WHAT! YOU'RE WEARING A SUIT! WERE WE SUPPOSED TO DRESS UP!?

YES, OF COURSE! DIDN'T SHE TELL YOU?

MAYBE SHE DID AND MAYBE I DIDN'T LISTEN

But fortunately...

YOU SHOULD WEAR THIS ONE! IT WILL SUIT YOU.

REALLY? I CAN REALLY WEAR THAT?

YES, AND YOU CAN WEAR THIS FUR STOLE OVER IT.

So there we were, wearing our dresses, drinking our cocktails and watching those lucky people on TV.

UGH! I HATE HER, SHE LOOKS SO WEIRD!

LOOK AT THAT FAKE NOSE!

IT LOOKS LIKE SHE HAS NO NOSE AND SHE HAD A WHOLE NEW PROSTHETIC NOSE BUILT FROM SCRATCH

There was a gossip contest and I learned shocking things about some stars.

SO IN THE HOTEL ROOM SHE COMES OUT OF THE BATHROOM, AND HE'S ALREADY UNDRESSED, AND-

WAIT, THEY GO STRAIGHT TO THE HOTEL? THEY DIDN'T GO ON LIKE A DATE?

OH, GABRIELLE...

It is a sad thing to watch the Oscars. I've gotten past the point where I can dream about ever attending them. The likelihood is almost zero percent, especially since I'm not interested in making a movie, though I'm still interested in attending the Oscars.

WHO ARE YOU WEARING?

SALVATION ARMY.

So we drink our cocktails, eat cake and envy those people who could've been us.

IS IT WEIRD THAT I DON'T LIKE HER? ISN'T SHE SOMEONE I'M SUPPOSED TO LIKE?

YEAH, SHE'S NOT MY TYPE EITHER.

we had a costume change.

march 14th

Me and Jenni took the subway out to the Cortelyou station on the Q for a Sunday tarot reading brunch. Jenni read aloud to me from the introduction to the Tennessee Williams play she was reading.

THE SINCERE REMARK IS FOLLOWED BY A CYNICAL DISTRUST. TRUTH IS FRAGMENTARY AT BEST. WE LOVE AND BETRAY EACH OTHER NOT QUITE IN THE SAME BREATH BUT IN TWO BREATHS THAT OCCUR IN FAIRLY CLOSE SEQUENCE. BUT THE FACT THAT PASSION OCCURED IN *PASSING*, THEN DECLINED INTO A MORE FAMILIAR SENSE OF INDIFFERENCE, SHOULD NOT BE REGARDED AS PROOF OF ITS INCONSEQUENCE.

WAIT, WHAT?

I wasn't doing so good. I had a sore throat and had been out till four in the morning playing pool with French men.

THAT'S IT, MELLOW AND DELICATE...

Why was I behaving like such a teenager? Just because one of the French men told me I was beautiful.

WHAT IS WITH THIS MUSEEK!

I KNOW! THE LEAST THEY COULD DO IS PLAY SOME LYNYRD SKYNYRD OR CREEDENCE!

Me and Jenni, for some reason, began hanging out on holidays. First Christmas, then New Year's, then her birthday, then the Super Bowl. On Valentine's day we went to a Polish restaurant and she read me a poem:

BUILD A WALL AROUND YOUR HEART, SO THAT LOVE CAN NEVER GET IN.

LOVE IS CRUELER THAN THE KNIFE OF A MAN WHO SLIT THE THROATS OF FOUR CHILDREN.*

* by Richard Brautigan

Out there in Flatbush the sun shone so brightly and the neighborhood was so affluent it felt like three hundred miles from New York.

THIS PLACE MAKES ME WANNA BREAK INTO SONG!

I JUST WANNA THROW MY ARMS AROUND THAT JOGGER AND KISS HIM!

(OOPS, DID HE HEAR ME?)

The brunch was something special. I was sick and on three hours of sleep but my mind was like damp clay, taking a cast of everything.

IN PARIS YOU CAN GET A TAROT READING FROM JODOROWSKI, AND THEN HE WILL MAKE YOU DRESS UP LIKE YOUR MOTHER OR SOMETHING.

I LIKE HOW THAT CENTERPIECE IS THE ONE TACKY THING IN THIS HOUSE. SOMEONE'S GRANDMA MUST'VE BROUGHT IT.

YOU'RE SO FUNNY.

Fumetto-Internationales Comix-Festival Luzern
Lucerne, Switzerland,
March 23rd - April 1st, 2012

Friday, March 23, 2012

Sometimes I wonder if we're actually living in a dystopian future horror situation like in 1984 and don't even know it.

But then I think, I'm capable of thinking, right? And of friendship, and love, and happiness, right? I think? So, that's something.

I didn't do much on the plane, just watched a movie about Carl Jung's Pygmalion-style relationship with his sexy, insane, kinky patient/mistress and some other bullshit.

In Zurich I met up with Vanessa who'd been traveling twice as long as me and together we tried to take the train to Lucerne.

But first we decided to take a random trip in the opposite direction to Berne for no particular reason.

So we lost three hours and thirty-three francs, but we did our best to put a positive spin on things. Also we got to take the scenic route.

THEY PROBABLY PUT EVERYBODY TO WORK SCRUBBING A FILTHY APARTMENT THIS MORNING AND THEY'LL BE FINISHING UP JUST AS WE ARRIVE.

WE'LL SHOW UP RIGHT ON TIME FOR THE CHAMPAGNE LUNCHEON ON THE BOAT.

We were met at the train station by Marcel, one of the festival's organizers, and his bike.

Crossing the Rathaus bridge, I saw two swans perform three perfectly synchronized loop-de-loops, followed by two expertly executed pirouettes. Then one lifted the other into the air and they flew off. But no one else saw it.

OMIGOD, DID YOU SEE THAT?

YEAH, THE SWANS ARE PRETTY, AREN'T THEY?

We arrived just in time for lunch, and to meet the women from Strapazin, the magazine whose issue featuring comics by women brought us there. I knew this was my one chance to make a good first impression but I just wouldn't take it.

WE FELT PRETTY DUMB BUT THEN WE GOT TO TAKE THE SCENIC ROUTE AND SEE ALL THE MOUNTAINS & FARMS. WE SAW LLAMAS!

MUNCH MUNCH

Saturday, March 24th

In the morning we went to the Raymond Pettibon Vernissage. All the women from Strapazin Magazine were around so it was like Vanessa and me instantly had a gang to hang with.

I LIKE YOUR RUSSIAN SCARF!

HOW DID YOU KNOW IT WAS RUSSIAN?

THANKS!

I CAN TELL BY THE DESIGNS!

SOMEHOW WE END UP TALKING ABOUT CLOTHES WHENEVER WE GET TOGETHER!

IT'S NOT JUST CLOTHES! IT'S TRADITIONAL RUSSIAN FOLK ART!

During the interview I had a sudden violent coughing fit. Have you ever tried to suppress a cough? It makes it much worse, you start gagging and tearing up.

IN THE EIGHTIES YOU BEGAN TO WORK IN COLLAGE. IS THIS BECAUSE COLLAGE REPRESENTS THE FRAGMENTATION OF OUR SOCIETY?

HYUNK HYUNK

Later we did a signing, but no one has heard of me in Lucerne. Except for this one lady. She printed out each of our photos from the internet for us to sign. The one of Sharmila was actually someone else. I don't know how she could have read my work since none of my books are translated into German, and she spoke no English.

VANESSA DAVIS?!!

NO, THAT'S VANESSA!

I drew her portrait, and it made her so happy. She made me happy. Fans need artists, and artists need fans.

HA HA!

Next there was a long opening/awards ceremony in German.

WHAT'S SO FUNNY? WHAT'D HE SAY?!

IT'S KINDA HARD TO EXPLAIN.

HA HA HA HA HA HA HA HA HA HA HA HA HA HA HA HA HA HA HA HA

Later Aisha Franz DJ'd a dance party with MTV videos projected on the wall. We were too tired to do much else but dance for hours to our beloved tween favorites. Sometimes it seems like dancing and drawing are the only things worth doing.

LADIES WITH AN ATTITUDE, FELLAS THAT WERE IN THE MOOD

Monday, March 26th (I'm skipping Sunday, it was just a gray hungover Sunday)

We went on the traditional Fumetto boatride around Lake Lucerne, a boat full of artists and their sketchbooks. I felt so gloomy I wanted to throw myself overboard.

THAT BIG HOUSE IS WHERE WAGNER LIVED.

THAT HOUSE WAS OWNED BY AUDREY HEPBURN.

SOME DAY THEY'LL SAY THAT ABOUT US CARTOONISTS.

(THAT'S ME)

Yes, it's true. I was in a cartoonist's paradise and all I felt was depressed.

...ESPECIALLY IF THIS BOAT SANK. ALL THIS TALENT GOING DOWN ALL AT ONCE. THEY'D HAVE A MEMORIAL FOR US EVERY YEAR.

It was frustrating being unable to discuss the stories in Strapazin because it was in German.

HOW MUCH OF YOUR STORY WAS AUTOBIOGRAPHICAL?

I'D SAY THE LAST THREE PAGES ARE SEMI-AUTOBIOGRAPHICAL.

I felt so mute, I envied everyone's easy rapport. How did they do it? For me, forming a sentence was a struggle, and gathering the momentum for a full conversation seemed impossible. Instead I focused on a drawing in a copy of Strapazin we were passing around for Kristiina.

Kristiina made it possible for a bunch of us to go to the Swedish Small Press Expo. She'd been kind to me when I was feeling similarly mute in Stockholm. She never received the magazine because she died of cancer, which I didn't know she had, a couple days later.

On the boat we met François Olisaeger and his fiancée Gabriela, who invited us to hang out at François' exhibition. I continued to be quiet, except to talk with Gabriela about the translating work she's doing for the Union of Concerned Scientists.

THERE ARE GLOBAL WARMING REFUGEES. PEOPLE HAVE TO LEAVE THEIR VILLAGES ON SMALL ISLANDS BECAUSE THE WATER IS RISING. AND MEANWHILE THE U.S. WON'T SIGN THIS TREATY, THOUGH THEY'RE THE BIGGEST POLLUTERS.

That evening we went out to dinner and I suddenly became talkative.

THERE WAS THIS GUY, AND HE WOULDN'T EAT ANY FLUFFY FOOD—

WHEN I WAS SIXTEEN I HAD A MOUSE NAMED GERALD WHO I KEPT IN MY POCKET, AND ONE TIME I PLAYED A TRICK ON MY LITTLE STEPSISTER, WHO LOVED GERALD. I BROUGHT A PLASTIC MOUSE TO OUR CHRISTMAS PARTY AND I PULLED IT OUT OF MY POCKET AND DIPPED IT IN SOME CREAMY DIP AND PUT IT IN MY MOUTH AND CHEWED IT. TO THIS DAY, SHE WON'T EAT ANYTHING CREAMY, NOT EVEN ICE CREAM.

ARE YOU TRYING TO SHOCK US?

## March 27th

This entry is dedicated to Dominique Goblet. I first met her when she sat on the chair next to me, the one I'd been using as a table to hold my glass of wine. She insisted on holding it for me.

NO PLEASE, I CAN TAKE MY CUP!

I MUST HOLD IT, BECAUSE I TOOK YOUR TABLE. IT'S NO PROBLEM, YOUR GLASS IS HERE FOR YOU WHENEVER YOU WANT A SIP. IT'S FITTING, SINCE MY NAME IS GOBLET.

Vanessa and I kept trying to figure out which superstar she looked like. That was before we learned that she was a truly great artist.

ELLEN PAGE?
BJORK?
PARKER POSEY?
MARY LOUISE PARKER?

When we saw her lecture, it felt like she was speaking only to me.

THE BIGGEST PROBLEM OF COMICS IS THE *LIGNE CLAIRE*.✳ THERE IS NO CLEAR LINE. IT'S A STEREOTYPE OF THE LEFT BRAIN.

AND THERE IS NO AUTOBIOGRAPHY BECAUSE THERE IS NO TRUENESS. THERE ARE FACTS AND THE LINKS THAT CONNECT THE FACTS.

✳(clear line, like Tintin)

And she was so open about herself. I thought, is it really possible to be that open, not to hide behind something, not to retreat behind some idea of discretion or shyness or modesty?

I NEEDED TO DO A BOOK ABOUT MY VIOLENT CHILDHOOD, BUT IT WASN'T JUST ABOUT BEING ABUSED. MY MOTHER WAS A VIOLENT PERSON, BUT I LOVED HER, AND SHE WAS NOT A MONSTER. EVERYONE IN THE STORY, INCLUDING THE CHILD, THAT IS, ME, PLAYED A COMPLICATED ROLE IN THE SITUATION.

Later Vanessa invited her over for dinner at the dorm-style apartment where we were staying. I wanted all her attention to myself. But what would I do with it if I had it?

I GREW UP IN CALIFORNIA, WHERE VANESSA LIVES NOW, AND I LIVE IN NEW YORK.

I USED TO LIVE IN NEW YORK, THAT'S WHERE WE MET.

YOU'RE BOTH AMERICANS!? ALL THIS TIME I THOUGHT YOU WERE GERMAN AND I WONDERED HOW YOU MANAGED TO SPEAK SUCH GOOD ENGLISH!!!

Then our new roommate came in, and without a word, turned on the tv and started to watch a football game.

WOULD YOU LIKE SOME VIENETTA?

WOULD YOU LIKE ME TO TURN OFF THE MUSIC?

YA.

YA.

Wednesday, March 28th

There was not much to be done that day so I set out in the direction of some woods, like a savage returning to its natural habitat.

It was crazy beautiful out there! The farther I walked, the more beautiful it got, so I walked for hours.

I thought about how after the inevitable economic and ecological collapse in the near future, maybe I could build a little shack from the detritus of our ruined civilization, and maybe I'd need to learn to kill people for my own survival.

THUD

But maybe I'd turn out to be good at killing, and maybe I'd get used to it. So maybe I'd be happy out there, except for the times I'd have to kill people. And sometimes during hard times I'd be forced to eat them, too, and that'd make me really sad, because they'd taste gross.

GARGH!!!
GAAH!!!
STAB!

I walked till my whole body was wobbling. I was thirsty and hungry but it didn't bother me because I was happy.

EDELWEISS

That night we went to the Jazz-kantin and I got a little drunk and talked a little trash.

SO HE COMES IN AND TURNS ON THE TV AND VANESSA'S LIKE, 'DO YOU WANT SOME VIENETTA', AND HE'S LIKE,'YA!'

I THINK I'LL TAKE HIS VIRGINITY!

Thursday, March 29th

Getting lost trying to find François' vernissage, I was accosted by a drunk guy.

YOU'RE LOOKING FOR FUMETTO?

YOU'RE AMERICAN?

FUNNY, I JUST MET SOMEONE FROM MISSISSIPPI. HE WAS, WHAT YOU CALL IT, "BLACK AMERICAN?" "U.S. BLACK."

HE WAS U.S. AFRICAN.

He creeped me out and I ran away.

WHERE ARE YOU GOING?

DON'T WORRY, I WON'T HURT YOU.

FUMETTO IS THAT WAY.

At the vernissage I felt morbidly shy, because Vanessa and the gang had all left. I felt so shy I had to walk around a corner into a deserted alley nearby just out of sight.

GULP GULP

I couldn't hide forever so I went ahead and steamrolled my way into a conversation.

HI.

HI!

WHAT ARE YOU GUYS TALKING ABOUT?

HE HAS SOME FRIENDS WHO LIVE IN THE TOWN WHERE I LIVE.

Then I was accosted again.

I'VE BEEN IN THE STATES I WENT IN THE FORESTS IN WASHINGTON AND I WENT TO THE BIG CRATER IN ARIZONA AND I WENT IN A SPACE SHUTTLE IN FLORIDA.

THEY CALL HIM MR. VERNISSAGE BECAUSE HE'S AT EVERY VERNISSAGE JUST FOR THE WINE. HE'S ALWAYS THE FIRST TO ARRIVE AND THE LAST TO LEAVE.

Later...

Hanging out at the crowded Jazzkantin, taking up a whole big table alone, pretending I don't care that I'm all by myself.

But then a bunch of artists joined me.

I'M GLAD YOU ARE DRAWING, THAT MEANS I CAN DRAW TOO.

WE SHOULD DO A DRAWING ROULETTE!

A drawing roulette is where we pass around our sketchbooks and build a drawing in each one collaboratively. I was anxious because I thought I had to be clever or slick.

DON'T THINK ABOUT IT! JUST DRAW!

IT'S TOO LATE, I'M AREADY THINKING ABOUT IT.

When I learned that the point was actually to be dumb I had the most fun I ever had drawing.

SWITCH!

DRAW DRAW DRAW DRAW DRAW DRAW DRAW

I don't want to forget that feeling. I'm afraid I'm going to spend the rest of my life looking for people to draw roulettes with.

THAT WAS SO FUN! CAN WE DO IT AGAIN?

YOU KNOW WHAT'S REALLY FUN IS WHEN TWO PEOPLE DO A PORTRAIT OF ANOTHER PERSON.

Then it was like we were one person, going around drawing everyone at the bar. We drew François Olisaeger and Serge Clerk and they drew us back.

IT'S LIKE, JUMPING OVER YOUR OWN SHADOW... IS THAT THE EXPRESSION? OR JUMPING ABOVE YOUR OWN SHADOW?

WE ARE A GENIUS!

Friday, March 30th

Over the city of Lucerne looms the newly renovated luxury hotel Château Gütsch, known to have hosted famous figures such as Charlie Chaplin, Queen Victoria and Julie Doucet, who, as legend has it, always had to leave the Fumetto parties early in order to catch the last cable car up the mountain.

I set out with my new drawing roulette friends Jared and Silvio in that direction.

(SWISS GERMAN)

WHAT ARE YOU GUYS TALKING ABOUT? "WHY DOES THIS IDIOT WANT TO GO TO THE GÜTSCH BUILDING"?

We stopped along the way at the art supply store where I got pens and paper that I couldn't get in the states.

WHAT IF I FOUND A MAGIC PEN AND EVERY-THING I DREW WITH IT WAS SO FANTASTIC I'D GET RICH AND FAMOUS AND THEN I LOST THE PEN AND DIED IN OBSCURITY.

WHAT IF ANY PEN DID THAT? THE PRISON IS IN YOUR OWN MIND.

IN THAT CASE I HAVE RECIDIVISM.

Silvio went off to meet somebody and Jared and I drew in the woods behind the Gütsch building.

I FEEL LIKE MY DRAWING STYLE HAS CHANGED OVER-NIGHT.

I FEEL LIKE MINE CHANGES EVERY DAY!

That night at the Jazzkantin I just wanted to do collaborative drawing again, but no one else was interested. It was like everyone had grown up and I perversely remained a child.

But I got Silvio to translate some stories from Strapazin instead.

"AS THE... -WHAT'S THE WORD FOR THE... PAINS OF THE CHILDBIRTH?

CONTRACTIONS?

YES, THAT'S IT. "AS THE CONTRAC-TIONS GOT CLOSER TOGETHER"-

DO IT IN A GIRLY VOICE!

"AS THE CONTRAC-TIONS GOT CLOSER TOGETHER..."

Saturday, March 31st

I love to hear Gabriela talk about her translating work for the U.o.C.S.

THE STATES ARE THE WORST! THERE'S NO REGULATION ON ALL THOSE COWS PRODUCING METHANE GAS, AND THEY WON'T SIGN THIS DAMNED TREATY! AT FIRST I THOUGHT SOMETHING COULD BE CHANGED. NOW I'M THINKING, I SHOULDN'T HAVE CHILDREN, AND I MIGHT AS WELL SMOKE!

We were just sorta hanging out till the big party would start later on.

HAVE YOU SEEN THIS COMIC, PARTYCAT? IT'S SO DUMB BUT IT'S BRILLIANT. IT'S JUST A CAT WHO WANTS TO PARTY ALL THE TIME.

HAHA! AND "PARTYING" IS JUST SORTA WAVING HIS PAWS AROUND AND BEING SURROUNDED BY BALLOONS. IS THAT THE TRICK? TO START WITH THE SIMPLEST, DUMBEST PREMISE AND GO FROM THERE?

OK, MY COMIC'S GONNA BE: "THE ON-AND-OFF TROUBLED RELATIONSHIP BETWEEN SALT AND PEPPER."

SALT... I'VE BEEN THINKING. I THINK WE SHOULD TRY HAVING AN OPEN RELATIONSHIP.

WELL, I'VE BEEN CHEATING ON YOU WITH THE CURRY, SO, SURE.

At the party I talked with Chippie, another member of Jared and Silvio's studio, Blackyard, which I've become a groupie of.

DO YOU GUYS EVER GET IN FIGHTS? DO YOU GET JEALOUS OF EACH OTHER?

WELL SURE, BUT WE WORK IT OUT.

Whenever there is dancing at a party, I always feel duty-bound to participate. It is not easy to dance all night long, but someone's gotta do it.

At five in the morning the fluorescent lights went on and turned the festive party into an army of ghoulish monsters.

DO YOU WANT SOME WATER?

I TRY TO DRINK AS LITTLE WATER AS POSSIBLE. DO YOU KNOW THE GERMAN TERM WELTSCHMERZ?

NO?

IT MEANS SOME-THING LIKE, 'ALL THE SAD-NESS OF THE WORLD.'

I HAVE A THEORY THAT THE WELT-SCHMERZ IS IN THE WATER.

Sunday, April first

*Last day of the festival.*

HEY GABRIELLE! WE'RE HAVING DINNER TONIGHT AT AROUND EIGHT. DO YOU WANT TO COME?

BUT POPEYE'S GODDA BLUES IS AT EIGHT!

Marcel

Eind

On the way to the theater to see Popeye's Godda Blues, I went in the complete wrong direction. The problem was, I couldn't ask anybody.

SORRY... DAS KLEIN THEATRE?

SORRY... DAS KLEIN THEATRE?

SORRY, WE'RE TOURISTS LIKE YOU.

DAS KLEIN WAS!?

After several tries someone finally took pity on me.

OH, YOU'RE LOOKING FOR THE KLEIN TAY-AH-TRUH. YOU ARE ABOUT A TWENTY MINUTE WALK FROM THERE. I'LL SHOW YOU, HERE IS WHERE WE ARE, AND OVER HERE IS THE KLEIN-TAY-AH-TRUH.

I arrived half an hour late.

THE PLAY IS HALF OVER. I CAN'T LET YOU IN, BUT IF YOU WANT YOU CAN WATCH IT FROM UP-STAIRS, I'LL SHOW YOU.

Popeyes Godda blues

THERE YOU GO.

GABRIELLE! I'M GLAD YOU COULD MAKE IT.

I'M SORRY I'M LATE, I—

YES, YOU'RE LATE!

It was a strange musical Swiss-German reinterpretation of an American comic strip. But the question is: would it have been better to have arrived on time and seen the whole thing with the rest of the audience, or to see only half of it from the special balcony with Marcel?

THE GUY THAT'S PLAYING POPEYE - BEAT-MAN - HE'S AN ICON IN SWITZERLAND, HE DOES CRAZY SHOWS AND RUNS AN INTER-NATIONAL RECORD LABEL. JACKIE, WHO'S PLAYING OLIVE OYL IS IN THE BAND THE JACKETS...

I will miss Lucerne, with its country-sides and whose fountains you can drink from, or so I am told.

IT'S FRESH FROM THE MOUNTAINS!

REALLY?

IS SHE MESSING WITH ME?

At the airport, heading towards security check, while stuffing my liquids into a too-small plastic baggy, I dropped a twenty-five dollar bottle of ink.

SMASH!

The floor was on an incline, and the jet black liquid made its way down the big clean white hall.

At that moment I had the feeling that my entire life was one big folly.

INFORMAT

SOMEBODY JUST SPILLED A BOTTLE OF INK AROUND THE CORNER OVER THERE.

THANKS, I'LL SEND SOMEONE OVER TO CLEAN IT UP.

IT'S PERMANENT, SO THEY'LL NEED SOME BLEACH.

Last March I spent two idyllic weeks in Lucerne for a comics festival and then I spent another two weeks writing and drawing about it and I haven't been the same since.

I learned two important things there. The first was the game of drawing roulette, the feeling of being a cog in a human drawing machine, creating something greater than the sum of its parts.

SCRITCH SCRITCH

The second thing was walking in the woods, where I felt an exquisite clarity.

I CAN FINISH A WHOLE THOUGHT!

JUST THINK OF ALL THE THINGS I CAN THINK OUT HERE!

When I came back I realized how unhappy I was.

I'VE LOST MY TRAIN OF—

WHAT WAS I THINKING JUST NOW?

I'M SO CONFUSED... WHAT WAS I...?

I know what you're thinking: "Why is Gabrielle obsessed with happiness? Does it even exist? Or is it a fictional concept that nobody can actually grasp? And if it does exist, wouldn't the last way to get it be to grasp at it? And aren't there more important things to think of, like helping those less fortunate, for example?" To that I'd say I'm not getting any younger, and I'm growing greedy for happiness.

Back in the States I introduced drawing roulette to my friends, but it wasn't the same.

SWITCH!

WAIT, LEMME JUST FINISH THIS—

THERE WAS NO WAITING TO FINISH IN SWITZERLAND!

I know, I know: "Why can't Gabrielle just chill out and go with the flow?"

HOW ABOUT WE EACH CHANNEL A DIFFERENT ARTIST. I CHOOSE KIPPENBERGER.

I MEAN, THAT'S NOT HOW WE DID IT IN—

ENOUGH ABOUT SWITZERLAND!

And then there was the woods! I asked Steve to take me to the Catskills.

HOW ARE WE DOING ON THE GPS?

WE'RE DOING GOOD! THE BLUE DOT IS ON THE BLUE LINE!

YOU ARE REFRESHING IT, AREN'T YOU?

WAIT, WHAT?

"Wait, now who the hell is Steve?! Are we supposed to know who Steve is!? Why does she keep dropping new characters into her comics without even introducing them?"

YOU GOTTA CLICK THE LITTLE ARROW IN THE BOTTOM LEFT CORNER.

UH-OH. ARE THE CATSKILLS IN CONNECTICUT?

So we had a very late start on our eight mile hike to the top of the mountain.

STEVE! YOU PROMISED THERE'D BE NO BEARS!

I DON'T REMEMBER MAKING THAT PROMISE BUT I'LL TAKE YOUR WORD FOR IT.

DO NOT FEED THE BEARS

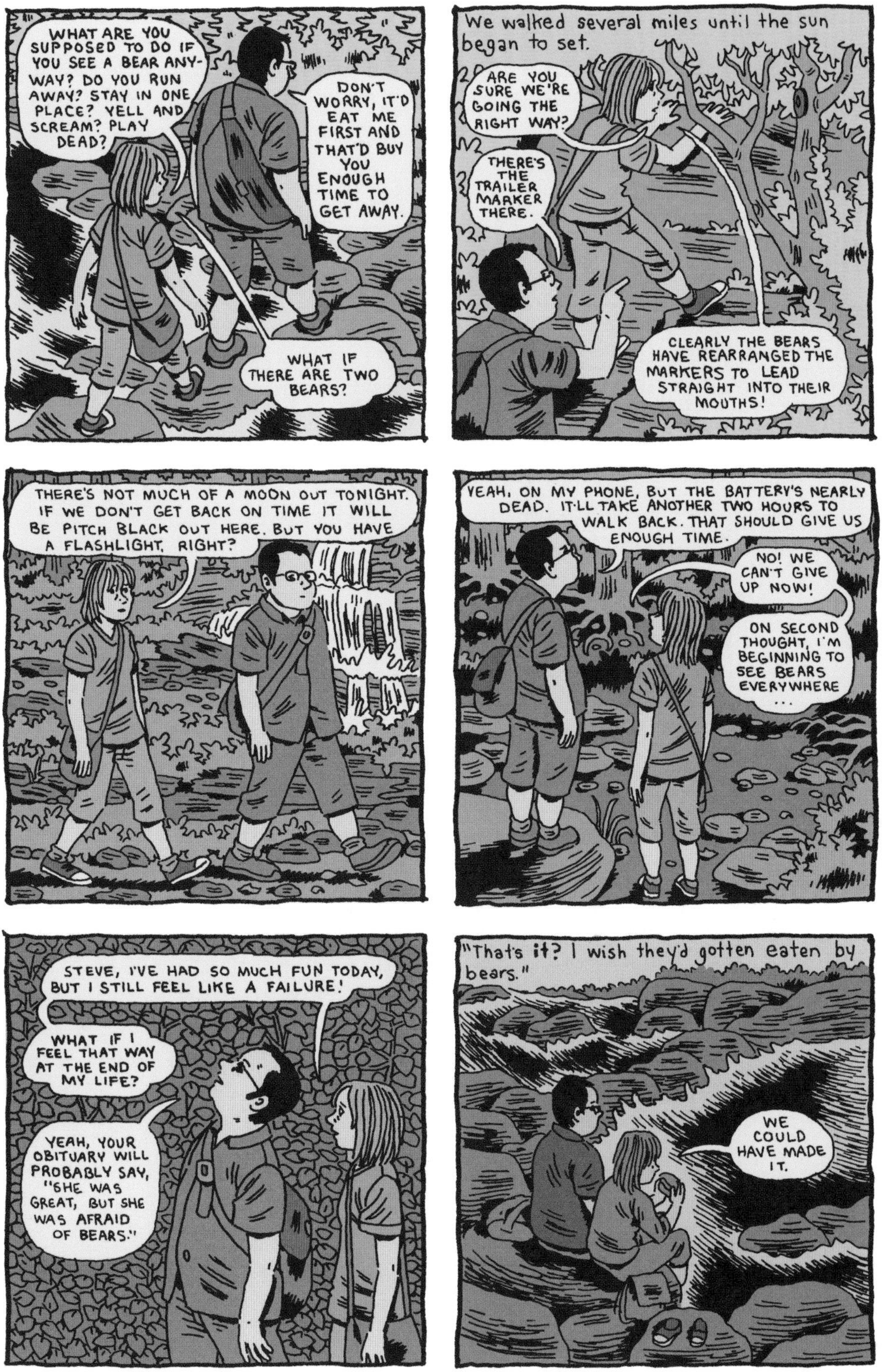
WHAT ARE YOU SUPPOSED TO DO IF YOU SEE A BEAR ANYWAY? DO YOU RUN AWAY? STAY IN ONE PLACE? YELL AND SCREAM? PLAY DEAD?
DON'T WORRY, IT'D EAT ME FIRST AND THAT'D BUY YOU ENOUGH TIME TO GET AWAY.
WHAT IF THERE ARE TWO BEARS?
We walked several miles until the sun began to set.
ARE YOU SURE WE'RE GOING THE RIGHT WAY?
THERE'S THE TRAILER MARKER THERE.
CLEARLY THE BEARS HAVE REARRANGED THE MARKERS TO LEAD STRAIGHT INTO THEIR MOUTHS!
THERE'S NOT MUCH OF A MOON OUT TONIGHT. IF WE DON'T GET BACK ON TIME IT WILL BE PITCH BLACK OUT HERE. BUT YOU HAVE A FLASHLIGHT, RIGHT?
YEAH, ON MY PHONE, BUT THE BATTERY'S NEARLY DEAD. IT'LL TAKE ANOTHER TWO HOURS TO WALK BACK. THAT SHOULD GIVE US ENOUGH TIME.
NO! WE CAN'T GIVE UP NOW!
ON SECOND THOUGHT, I'M BEGINNING TO SEE BEARS EVERYWHERE ...
STEVE, I'VE HAD SO MUCH FUN TODAY, BUT I STILL FEEL LIKE A FAILURE!
WHAT IF I FEEL THAT WAY AT THE END OF MY LIFE?
YEAH, YOUR OBITUARY WILL PROBABLY SAY, "SHE WAS GREAT, BUT SHE WAS AFRAID OF BEARS."
"That's it? I wish they'd gotten eaten by bears."
WE COULD HAVE MADE IT.

July 2012

## Sunday, July first, 2012

To be honest, I'm pretty nervous. How am I supposed to draw a comic about my monotonous, habit-driven, altogether too easy life without sounding boring, small-minded, annoying, repetitive?

Like a reality show for your sad old aunt you see once a year who spends her days exactly as you'd expect: reading romance novels and redecorating the living room.

Because in spite of what you might think, I don't have much of an inner life. For example: I have no favorite music. "What do you listen to on your ipod?" You might ask. I'd answer that I don't have an ipod. "Spotify?" No. "What do you listen to while you wander around the city by yourself?" I don't wander around the city. I sit quietly in a dark room and wait until I'm needed.

Anyway... I just got back from a business trip, first to Chicago, then LA, to attend conventions and try to persuade people to buy my new books.

In Chicago I stayed with Aaron Renier. Aaron is the kind of person who has no facebook account but has lots of real friends. On the last day of my visit we invented a game I'll call Zombie Apocalypse.

▮▮▮? WOULD YOU LET HIM LIVE?

WHAT ABOUT ▮▮▮?

SURE, HE COULD BE USEFUL. BUT NOT ▮▮▮ SHE'D SLOW US DOWN.

BUT WHAT IF THAT MADE ▮▮▮ SO BEREFT HE LOST HIS WILL TO FIGHT?

YOU'RE RIGHT. SHE COULD MAKE A GOOD HIVE MOTHER.

Zombie Apocalypse was very helpful in passing the long hours in traffic jams between LA and the Anaheim convention center with Tom K.

WOULD YOU REALLY LET ▮▮▮ DIE? WHERE IS YOUR LOYALTY?

HE'S DEAD WEIGHT! THIS IS NOT ABOUT LOYALTY, IT'S ABOUT SURVIVAL!

When I got home again and was idly poring through my news feed, I saw that people were discussing their zombie survival groups. Our game was already a meme! Is facebook stealing our inner lives?

Monday, July second

I worked all day yesterday. Yep, drawing comics about drawing comics. Except when Tony stopped in.

JENNI'S NEXT DOOR AT MY PLACE. SHE DIDN'T WANT TO BOTHER YOU BECAUSE SHE KNOWS YOU'RE BUSY WORKING.

BUT CAN SHE COME IN AND USE THE INTERNET FOR AWHILE?

Jenni was living in a big warehouse loft full of artists on the waterfront when it was suddenly condemned and they were all evicted.

The guy at Jenni's bodega offered to rent her his basement, but he turned out to be a loose cannon. He showed up with a couple of cronies to help her move and went nuts.

WHAT THE FUCK ARE YOU ALL STILL DOING HERE!? EVERYBODY GET THE FUCK OUT!

The loft was all cleared out but the old tenant hadn't moved out of the basement yet, so Jenni's new landlord gave her the keys to his own place, where she found a rottweiler named Zeus.

HI, BOY...

SNARL!...

I TRIED TO MAKE FRIENDS WITH HIM BUT HE SNAPPED AT ME. I WAS LIKE, I'M NOT MESSING WITH YOU, YOU'RE NAMED AFTER THE KING OF THE GREEK GODS!

I walked back with Jenni to her old place. She was going to either sleep there or at my apartment.

I DUNNO, JENNI. IT'S PRETTY CREEPY AND DARK HERE. IF IT WERE ME I WOULDN'T WANT TO SLEEP HERE ALONE.

SPATS! WE'VE ALL BEEN LOOKING FOR YOU!

MEOW!!

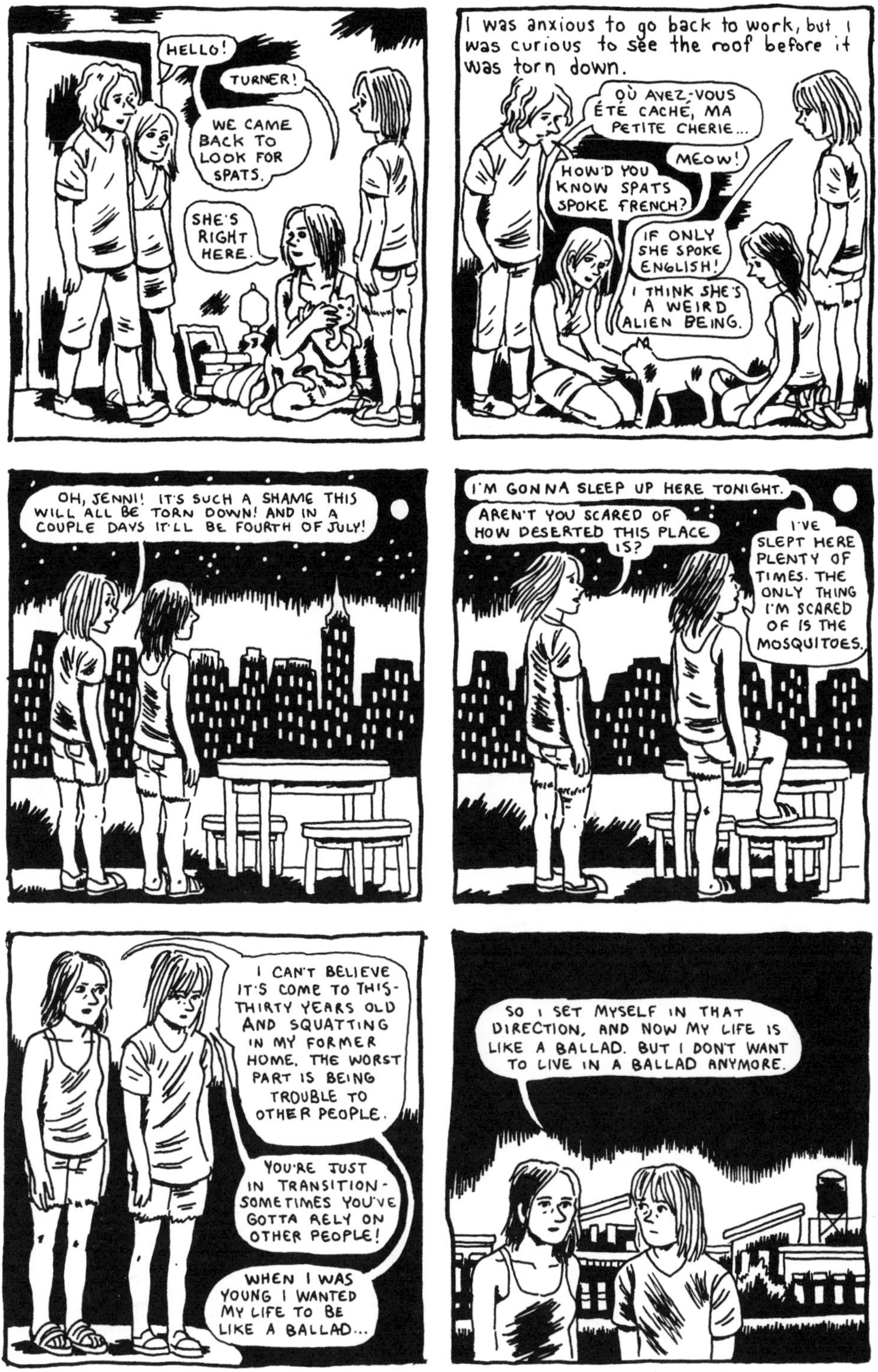
HELLO!
TURNER!
WE CAME BACK TO LOOK FOR SPATS.
SHE'S RIGHT HERE.
I was anxious to go back to work, but I was curious to see the roof before it was torn down.
OÙ AVEZ-VOUS ÉTÉ CACHÉ, MA PETITE CHERIE...
MEOW!
HOW'D YOU KNOW SPATS SPOKE FRENCH?
IF ONLY SHE SPOKE ENGLISH!
I THINK SHE'S A WEIRD ALIEN BEING.
OH, JENNI! IT'S SUCH A SHAME THIS WILL ALL BE TORN DOWN! AND IN A COUPLE DAYS IT'LL BE FOURTH OF JULY!
I'M GONNA SLEEP UP HERE TONIGHT.
AREN'T YOU SCARED OF HOW DESERTED THIS PLACE IS?
I'VE SLEPT HERE PLENTY OF TIMES. THE ONLY THING I'M SCARED OF IS THE MOSQUITOES.
I CAN'T BELIEVE IT'S COME TO THIS-THIRTY YEARS OLD AND SQUATTING IN MY FORMER HOME. THE WORST PART IS BEING TROUBLE TO OTHER PEOPLE.
YOU'RE JUST IN TRANSITION-SOMETIMES YOU'VE GOTTA RELY ON OTHER PEOPLE!
WHEN I WAS YOUNG I WANTED MY LIFE TO BE LIKE A BALLAD...
SO I SET MYSELF IN THAT DIRECTION, AND NOW MY LIFE IS LIKE A BALLAD. BUT I DON'T WANT TO LIVE IN A BALLAD ANYMORE.

It was getting late, but Steve texted, and he'd never seen this roof either.

THESE ROOFTOPS GO ON FOREVER!

LET ME SHOW YOU WHERE I CAMP...

YOU GUYS SHOULD SLEEP UP HERE WITH ME! IT'S YOUR LAST CHANCE!

WE CAN BRING BLANKETS AND CUSHIONS FROM DOWNSTAIRS.

LOOK AT THOSE PENTHOUSES. THEY PROBABLY PAY FIVE THOUSAND A MONTH FOR THAT TINY PORTION OF ROOF ACCESS.

YOU PAID SIX HUNDRED A MONTH FOR A WHOLE CITY BLOCK!

I COULD GROW AN ENTIRE FARM UP HERE.

YOU COULD RAISE COWS AND SHEEP! PASTURES! MILKMAIDS! SHEPHERDS!

WOLVES! WILD HORSES! ORCHARDS! SKI SLOPES!

IT'S LIKE A BEAUTIFUL UNTOUCHED ISLAND SINKING INTO THE SEA BEFORE OUR EYES!

IT'S CRAZY HOW WE'RE IN THE MIDDLE OF THE CITY, AND YET THERE'S THIS DEEP, QUIET, SPIRITUAL FEELING HERE.

STEVE, CAN YOU TAKE A PHOTO OF THIS WITH YOUR IPHONE? MAKE SURE YOU GET THE MOON IN IT, AND THE SKYLINE, AND THE MOONLIGHT ON THE RIVER, AND THE GENTLE BREEZE AND THE DISTANT SOUNDS OF THE CITY...

SURE, I'LL JUST USE MY "DEEP SPIRITUAL FEELING" APP.

WON'T YOU STAY HERE TONIGHT? IT'D BE SO FUN!

I DON'T THINK I'D BE ABLE TO SLEEP UP HERE...

YOU SLEEP EXTRA DEEP UNDER THE STARS! YOU WAKE UP AT DAWN COMPLETELY REFRESHED!

YOU COULD DO A COMIC ABOUT IT!

PEOPLE OFTEN SAY THAT TO GET ME TO DO THINGS. AND YOU KNOW, IT WORKS.

And so...

I'M GETTING EATEN ALIVE BY MOSQUITOES!

Wednesday, July Fourth

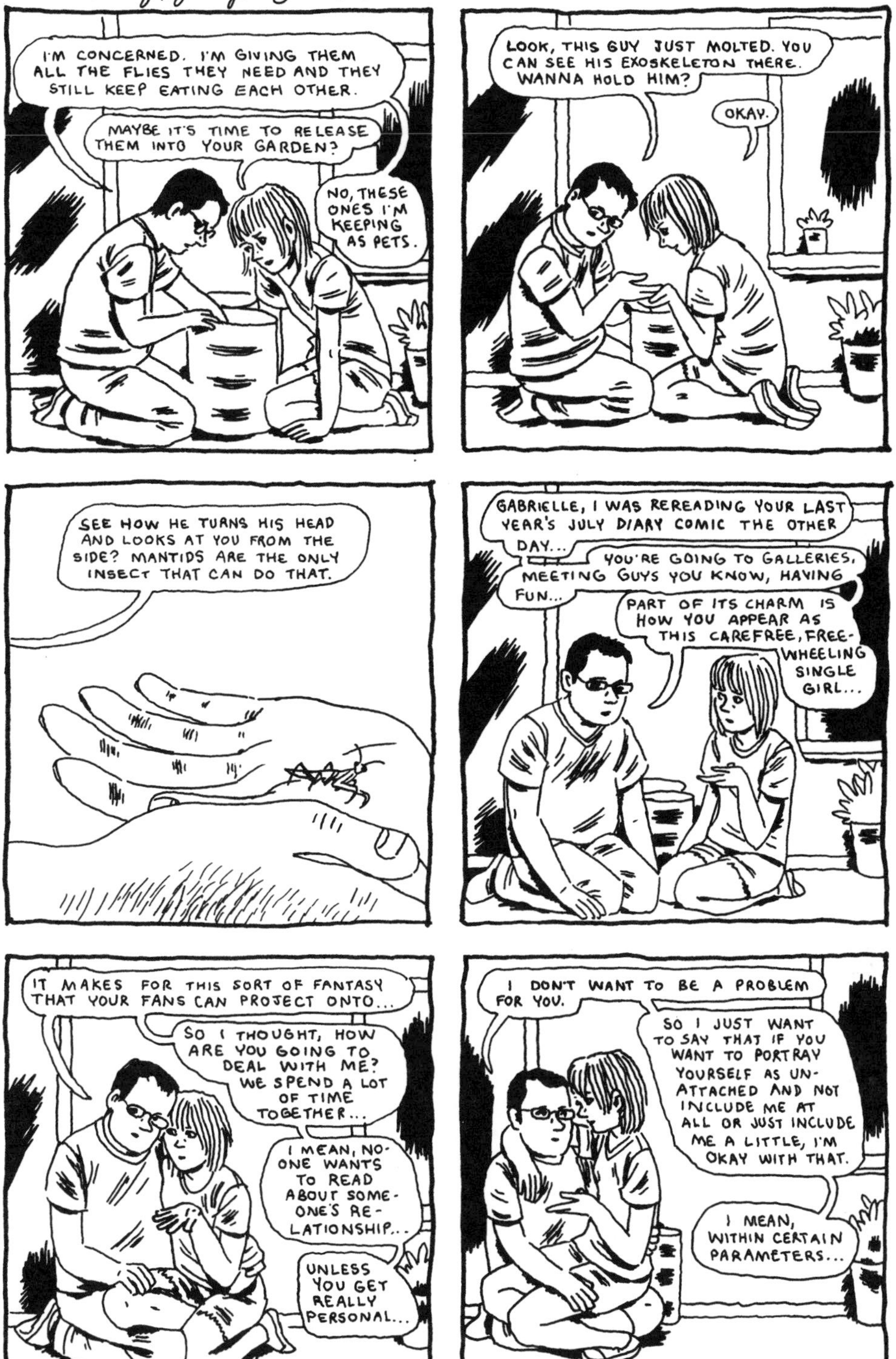
I'M CONCERNED. I'M GIVING THEM ALL THE FLIES THEY NEED AND THEY STILL KEEP EATING EACH OTHER.
MAYBE IT'S TIME TO RELEASE THEM INTO YOUR GARDEN?
NO, THESE ONES I'M KEEPING AS PETS.
LOOK, THIS GUY JUST MOLTED. YOU CAN SEE HIS EXOSKELETON THERE. WANNA HOLD HIM?
OKAY.
SEE HOW HE TURNS HIS HEAD AND LOOKS AT YOU FROM THE SIDE? MANTIDS ARE THE ONLY INSECT THAT CAN DO THAT.
GABRIELLE, I WAS REREADING YOUR LAST YEAR'S JULY DIARY COMIC THE OTHER DAY...
YOU'RE GOING TO GALLERIES, MEETING GUYS YOU KNOW, HAVING FUN...
PART OF ITS CHARM IS HOW YOU APPEAR AS THIS CAREFREE, FREE-WHEELING SINGLE GIRL...
IT MAKES FOR THIS SORT OF FANTASY THAT YOUR FANS CAN PROJECT ONTO...
SO I THOUGHT, HOW ARE YOU GOING TO DEAL WITH ME? WE SPEND A LOT OF TIME TOGETHER...
I MEAN, NO-ONE WANTS TO READ ABOUT SOME-ONE'S RE-LATIONSHIP...
UNLESS YOU GET REALLY PERSONAL...
I DON'T WANT TO BE A PROBLEM FOR YOU.
SO I JUST WANT TO SAY THAT IF YOU WANT TO PORTRAY YOURSELF AS UN-ATTACHED AND NOT INCLUDE ME AT ALL OR JUST INCLUDE ME A LITTLE, I'M OKAY WITH THAT.
I MEAN, WITHIN CERTAIN PARAMETERS...

# july fourth, continued

STEVE, DOES THIS DRESS MAKE ME LOOK TOO GORGEOUS?

EVERY TIME I WEAR A DRESS IN PUBLIC A VOICE IN MY HEAD GOES: "WHO DO YOU THINK YOU ARE? SOME KIND OF PRINCESS?"

IT IS YOUR DUTY TO THE COUNTRY TO BE PRETTY TODAY.

"SOME SPECIAL, PRETTY, PATRIOTIC, AMERICAN PRINCESS?"

FREE BOOKS

HI! DON'T YOU LOOK PRETTY!

DON'T *YOU* LOOK PRETTY!

HELEN, THIS IS STEVE, AND OUR WATER-MELON.

WHAT'S THAT BOOK YOU'VE GOT, STEVE?

IT'S A BOOK BY JANET LEIGH. SHE STARRED IN PSYCHO AND THEN SHE WROTE THIS ROMANCE NOVEL.

I JUST SAW THE REMAKE OF PSYCHO.

IT WAS SO BAD! THEY JUST RESHOT THE ORIGINAL, BUT LEFT OUT EVERY-THING THAT WAS GOOD ABOUT IT. WHY WOULD THEY DO THAT?

MAYBE TO LEARN TO MAKE A GOOD MOVIE?

YOU MEAN BY COPYING BIT BY BIT?

THEY DO THAT TO LEARN ABOUT WRITING. LIKE YOU'D COPY THE SUN ALSO RISES WORD BY WORD.

YOU CAN DO IT WITH COMICS TOO. AND BREAK DANCING!

THEN YOU'D HAVE A WHOLE NEW BOOK YOU CAN GIVE TO A FRIEND.

I COULD SEE THAT BEING A THING. THE SCRIBE'S CLUB. THEY MEET ONCE A YEAR TO EXCHANGE HAND-SCRIBED, REWRITTEN BOOKS!

I MEAN, IT'S NO WORSE THAN KNITTING!

OOOH!

BURN!

I'M MAKING MATCHING SLIPPERS FOR MY TWO LITTLE COUSINS.

IT'S A STITCH MY GRANDMOTHER TAUGHT ME.

OH! UM...

HELEN, WOULD YOU LIKE TO JOIN OUR ZOMBIE APOCALYPSE SURVIVAL GROUP?

Friday, July sixth

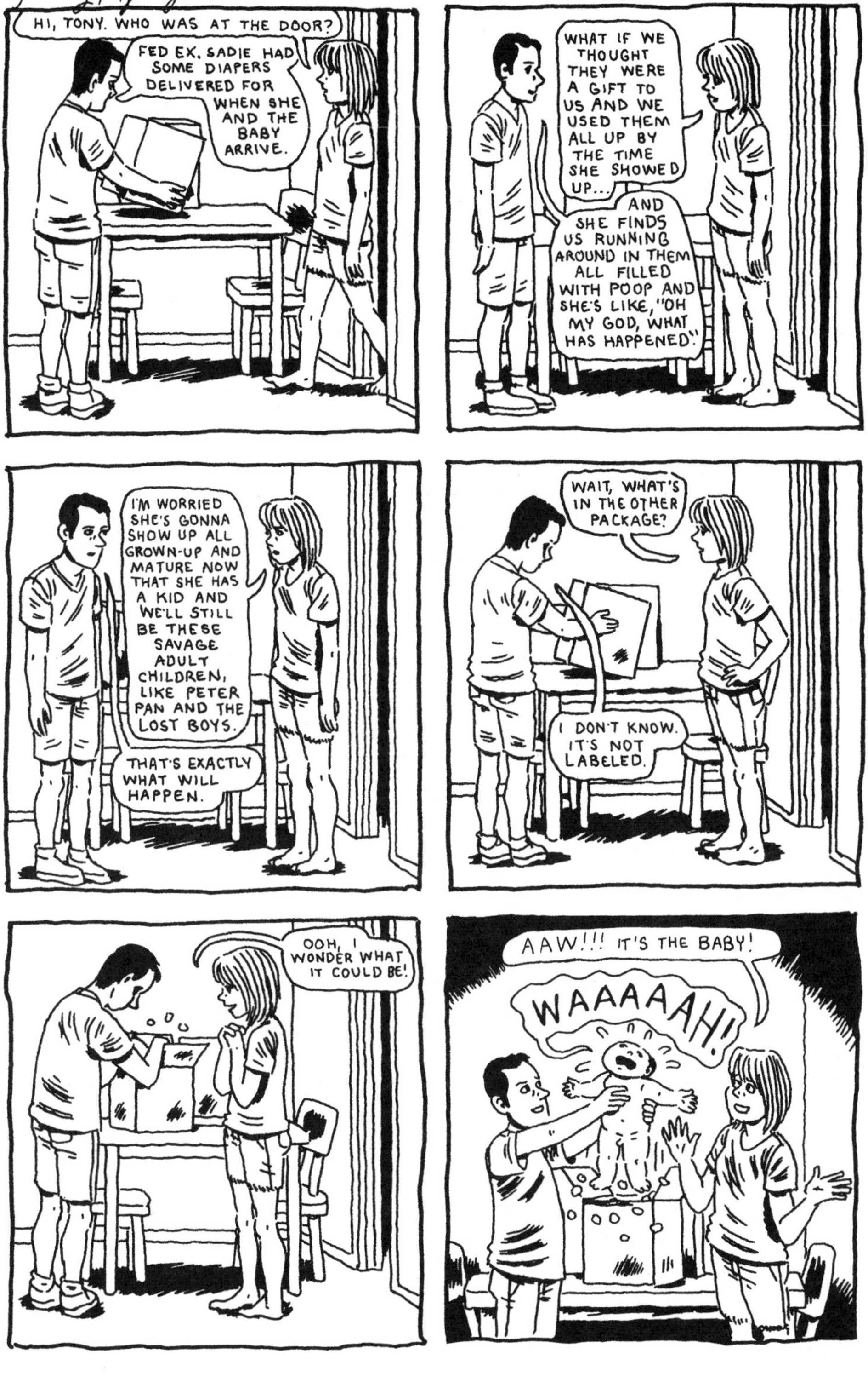
HI, TONY. WHO WAS AT THE DOOR?
FED EX. SADIE HAD SOME DIAPERS DELIVERED FOR WHEN SHE AND THE BABY ARRIVE.
WHAT IF WE THOUGHT THEY WERE A GIFT TO US AND WE USED THEM ALL UP BY THE TIME SHE SHOWED UP...
AND SHE FINDS US RUNNING AROUND IN THEM ALL FILLED WITH POOP AND SHE'S LIKE, "OH MY GOD, WHAT HAS HAPPENED."
I'M WORRIED SHE'S GONNA SHOW UP ALL GROWN-UP AND MATURE NOW THAT SHE HAS A KID AND WE'LL STILL BE THESE SAVAGE ADULT CHILDREN, LIKE PETER PAN AND THE LOST BOYS.
THAT'S EXACTLY WHAT WILL HAPPEN.
WAIT, WHAT'S IN THE OTHER PACKAGE?
I DON'T KNOW. IT'S NOT LABELED.
OOH, I WONDER WHAT IT COULD BE!
AAW!!! IT'S THE BABY!
WAAAAAH!

# Saturday, July seventh

At a party in the country.

"I'M RUNNING OUT OF THINGS TO SAY HERE. MAYBE I'LL GO JOIN THAT CONVERSATION."

"AT THE DOG PARK THEY'LL LOOK AT ME LIKE, 'HOW COULD YOU *DO* SUCH A THING?'"

"WHAT IF YOU USED HER FUR TO MAKE A COAT AND YOU WORE IT TO THE PARK..."

"YOU SAID THAT LIKE YOU WERE SEVEN YEARS OLD."

"YOU COULD DYE IT PURPLE AND HER TO MATCH..."

"ARE YOU SEVEN YEARS OLD?"

"LEANNE! I LOVE YOUR BATHROOM. ARE THOSE SEASHELLS?"

"YES! I HAD AN EIGHT AND TEN-YEAR-OLD OVER AND I PUT THEM TO WORK."

"I GUESS I'LL GO SEE WHAT MY CONTEMPORARIES HAVE BEEN UP TO."

LOCK!

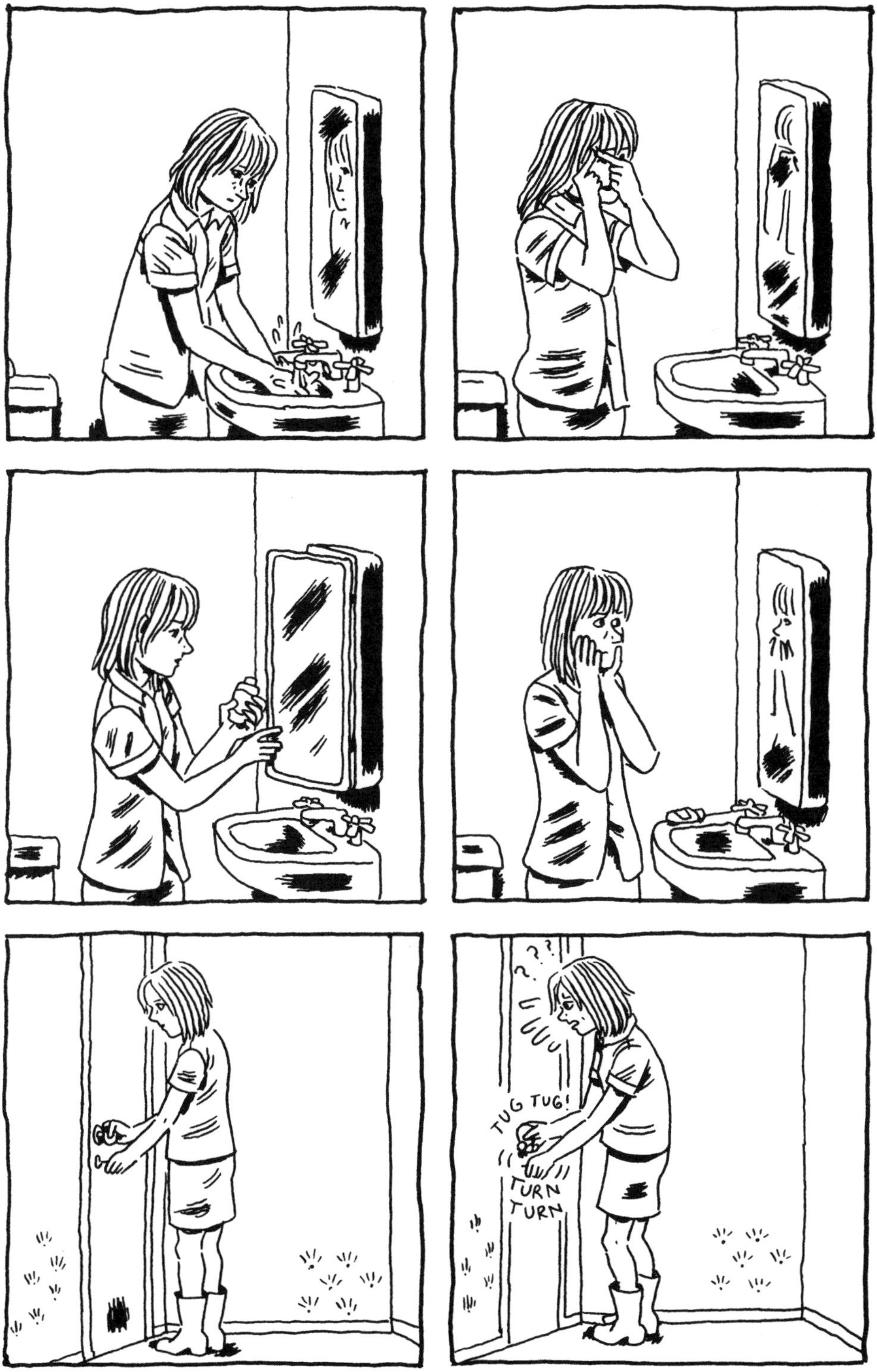
???
TUG TUG!
TURN TURN

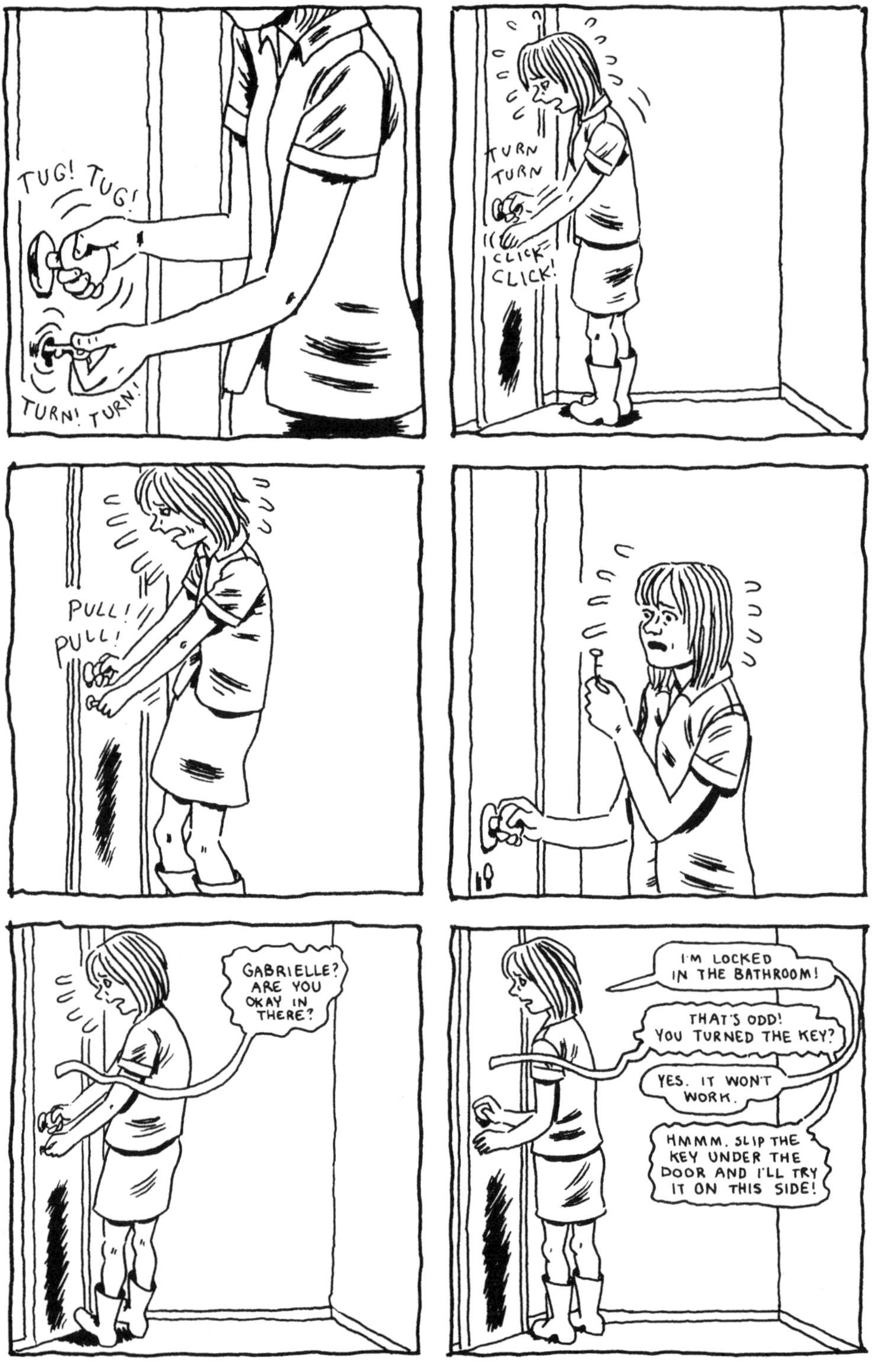
TUG! TUG!
TURN! TURN!
TURN
TURN
CLICK
CLICK!
PULL!
PULL!
GABRIELLE? ARE YOU OKAY IN THERE?
I'M LOCKED IN THE BATHROOM!
THAT'S ODD! YOU TURNED THE KEY?
YES. IT WON'T WORK.
HMMM. SLIP THE KEY UNDER THE DOOR AND I'LL TRY IT ON THIS SIDE!

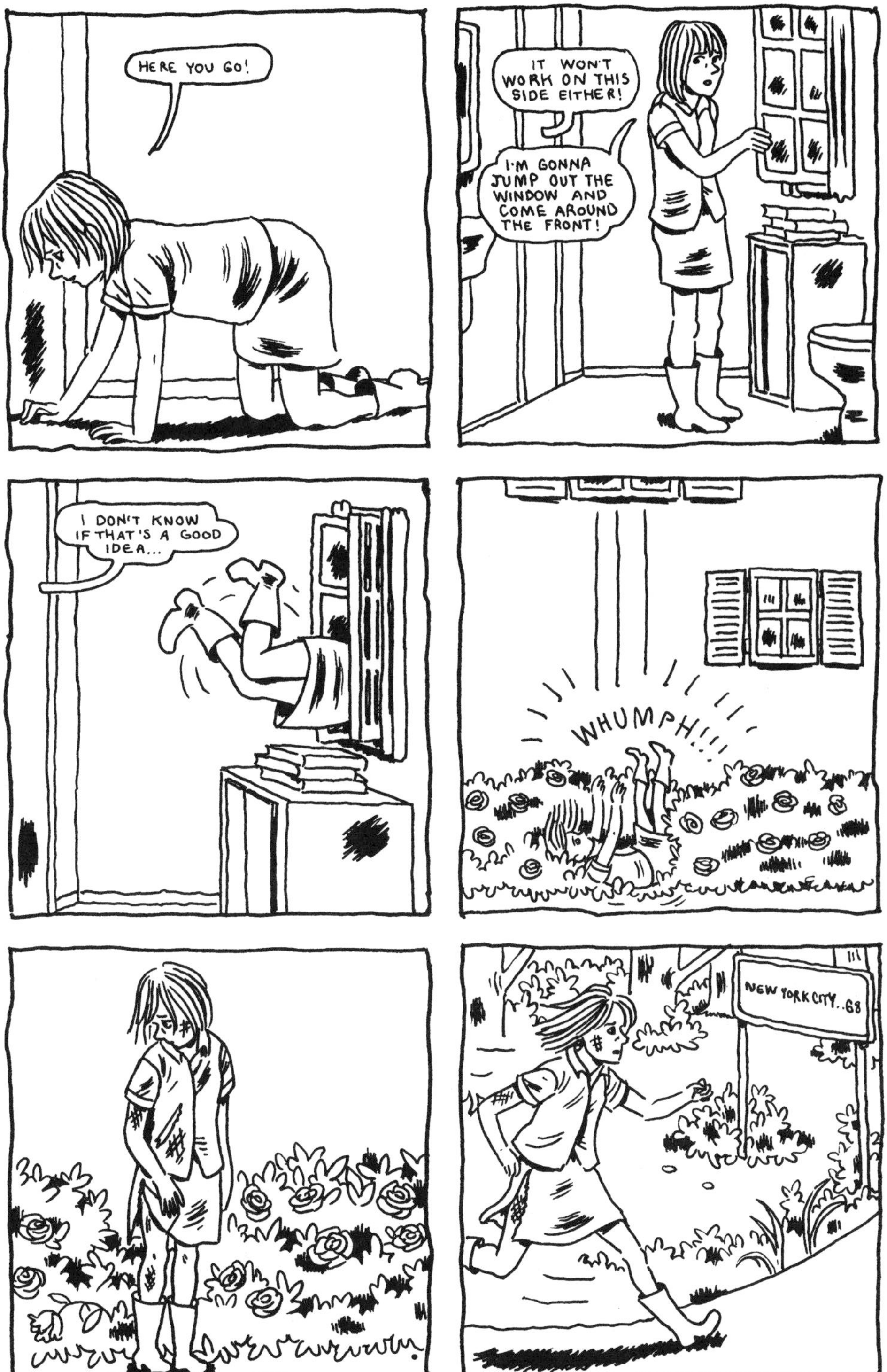
HERE YOU GO!
IT WON'T WORK ON THIS SIDE EITHER!
I'M GONNA JUMP OUT THE WINDOW AND COME AROUND THE FRONT!
I DON'T KNOW IF THAT'S A GOOD IDEA...
WHUMPH!!!
NEW YORK CITY..68

# Thursday, July twelfth

We went to the Catskills again. This time we meant to do it right. On the way there, we studied up on what to do about bears.

EXPECT TO FIND BEARS IN RIPE BLUEBERRY PATCHES. YOU CAN OFTEN SEE THEM DIGGING IN THE EARTH FOR INSECTS. THEY ESPECIALLY LIKE ANTS.

ANTS! THEY MUST BE LIKE POPPY-SEEDS TO THEM!

SO AN ANT ON A BLUE-BERRY MUST BE LIKE A REESE'S PEANUT BUTTER CUP.

WHAT TO DO IF YOU ENCOUNTER A BEAR: DO NOT RUN AWAY. DO NOT CORNER IT, DO NOT STARE. THESE THINGS WILL ENCOURAGE IT TO ATTACK YOU. BACK AWAY SLOWLY. TURN AT A 45 DEGREE ANGLE.

WHAT ABOUT ZOMBIE BEARS? I BET THERE'S A WHOLE DIFFERENT SET OF RULES FOR ZOMBIE BEAR ENCOUNTERS.

This time we made it to the top of the mountain. Also we saw a crashed air-plane.

I THOUGHT IT'D BE BIGGER.

WHAT, DID YOU EXPECT A 747, WITH SKELETONS STILL STRAPPED TO THE SEATS?

WHO WAS IN THE PLANE, ANYWAY?

IT WAS A VERY SAD STORY, ACTUALLY...

IT WAS A FAMILY... THE FATHER WAS AN OLYMPIC MEDALIST AND A VETERAN. HE WAS FLYING WITH HIS WIFE AND THEIR TWO SMALL CHILDREN, A BOY AND A GIRL...

HOW DID THEY CRASH?

I'M GETTING TO THAT... THE WIFE WAS PREGNANT WITH A THIRD CHILD, AND HER HUSBAND HAD FOUND OUT THAT THIS ONE WAS NOT HIS. THERE WAS A TERRIBLE ROW THAT ENDED IN TRAGEDY.

Everything was going fine until we ran out of water and got dehydrated and lost.

I JUST HALLUCINATED A WEIRD, FREAKY HELLHOUND-CREATURE OUT OF THE CORNER OF MY EYE.

OH, THAT? NO, I SEE IT TOO.

We stumbled onto an old abandoned road, and a familiar jingle reached our ears...

IS THAT WHAT I—

YES...

That's not exactly how it happened. We did run out of water, and we did make a wrong turn that brought us to another road, but Steve had a GPS device that made it impossible to get lost.

THAT LITTLE TRIANGLE IS US. WE'RE JUST OVER TWO MILES OUT OF OUR WAY.

WE'RE BARELY MOVING!

THAT'S BECAUSE WE AREN'T IN A CAR.

And an ice cream truck DID come around the bend, driven by a lady who could have stepped out of some quirky indie movie.

I'M GLAD TO SEE YOU GUYS! I'VE BARELY HAD ANY CUSTOMERS TODAY.

I ALSO HAVE GATORADE.

# Saturday, July fourteenth

After yoga class...

MY TEENAGE SON MADE ME STOP WEARING BAGGY CLOTHES BECAUSE IT WAS EMBARRASSING HIM.

HE GOT ME WEARING SKINNY JEANS.

REALLY!

HE'S KEEPING ME YOUNG!

AND HE SAID, 'MOM, DO SOMETHING WITH YOUR HAIR!'

SO I SHAVED IT ALL OFF! MAYBE THAT'S WHY I CAN'T FIND A BOYFRIEND.

I'M SURE THAT'S NOT THE PROBLEM.

ALL MY FAMILY IS SAYING, 'YOU'RE GETTING OLD! DO YOU WANT TO BE ALONE FOREVER?'

SO I GO OUT ON DATES, BUT THE MEN ARE ALL CRAZY!

I WENT OUT WITH THIS ONE GUY, HE WAS SO HANDSOME, HE WAS A BOXER, VERY BIG AND STRONG...

BUT ALL HE TALKED ABOUT WAS GOING TO THE GYM!

THEN THERE WAS THIS OTHER GUY, I HAD TO MEET HIM AFTER MY TAE-KWON DO CLASS...

SO I TOLD HIM, 'I WON'T BE SO PRETTY BECAUSE I WON'T HAVE TIME TO SHOWER OR PUT ON MAKE-UP,'

AND HE SAYS, 'THAT'S FINE...'

SO I SHOWED UP ALL SWEATY, WEARING BAGGY CLOTHES...

AND I NOTICED HIS HANDS AND HIS LEGS WERE CLEARLY TREMBLING...

HE WAS NERVOUS?

HE WAS HORNY! HE SUDDENLY STARTED HUGGING ME RIGHT THEN, AND I COULD FEEL HIS BULGE PRESSING UP AGAINST ME!

THIS WAS A TOTAL STRANGER! HOW COULD ANYONE DO THAT!?

HAVE YOU EVER HAD THE URGE TO DO SOMETHING LIKE THAT? TO SOMEONE YOU JUST MET!?

I'M MUCH TOO REPRESSED.

AND THEN THERE WAS THIS GUY I HAD TO DUMP BECAUSE HE COULDN'T PRONOUNCE MY NAME RIGHT...

CHANG-UN-SOOK? CHUNG-AN-SOOK?

MAYBE YOUR STANDARDS ARE TOO HIGH?

# Monday, July sixteenth

I scrubbed all the black mold from the bathtub.

Tony installed air conditioning and a diaper-changing table in the bedroom.

ARE YOU SURE THERE'S NOTHING I CAN DO TO HELP?

NO, YOU CAN GO BACK TO YOUR WORK.

PLEASE, ANYTHING BUT THAT!

And then we were at the airport where it took so long to get the complicated car seat in but who cares.

YOU GUYS GOTTA MOVE YOUR—OH, SORRY. TAKE YOUR TIME.

All this big dangerous machinery, the pieces put together, maintained and driven by flawed adult people, to carry this tiny, soft thing to my apartment.

I'M GONNA GO TO ANN ARBOR TO GET MY INSTRUCTOR'S PERMIT. TOBY'S GONNA WATCH—

OH MY GOD, HE'S LOOKING AT ME! IT'S UNBEARABLE! HE TIES MY HEART IN KNOTS!

Every gesture—a yawn—a smile—completely unhinges me.

ARE YOU TOTALLY INURED TO HIS ADORABLENESS BY NOW?

OH, I STILL LIKE HIM.

We were nearly run off the road by a "party bus," heading for Manhattan.

IS HE SPANKING HER UP THERE?

WHY PARTY IN A BUS ANY-WAY? CAN'T THEY WAIT TILL THEY GET TO WHERE THEY'RE GOING?

# Wednesday, July eighteenth

I had to rehearse my show for The Moon. This meant having to meet new people. It's hard to meet new people. What if they don't like me?

> HI.
>
> HI.
>
> THIS IS MISHU.

Or maybe it's not so hard.

> SORRY, I'VE GOT TO FINISH THIS—
>
> NO PROBLEM, I'LL JUST PLAY WITH MISHU.

Can these people see how frightened I am? Or do I appear cool? Or do I appear like I'm trying to be cool?

> GOT A CARE PACKAGE!
>
> Cool!

Or do I seem not cool at all, but vulnerable, flawed, non-threatening, likable?

> FANCY GOWNS! WHAT WILL I DO WITH THESE?
>
> WE COULD TRY TO START A TREND.

What if I was rich and famous? Would people like me more? Would they just tell themselves they liked me? Would I need to care?

> I WAS THINKING IT MIGHT BE FUNNY TO HAVE A GUY READ THE PART OF MY MOM.
>
> BUT WHAT WOULD THAT SAY IN A STORY ABOUT FEMINISM?
>
> TRUE...

Or would I hide away in an estate in Connecticut with my other rich and famous friends, and become even more afraid of the world?

> BUT THEN AGAIN, IT'D SHOW HER IN A NON-TRADITIONAL WAY IN TERMS OF GENDER.
>
> THAT'S TRUE TOO.

## Thursday, July nineteenth

Oh, man, I'm in no shape to draw a comic today. I am too worn out from trying on all my dresses.

Or maybe from this 100 degree un-air-conditioned heat.

But mostly it's from being so nervous about my SCUM Manifesto performance for The Moon show last night,

OKAY, LET'S DO A RUN-THROUGH! TIM, ARE YOU READY? CAMILLE, WHERE ARE YOU?

MAY I HAVE ANOTHER DRINK TICKET?

although I had nothing to be nervous about.

THE ONLY REMAINING MEMBERS WILL BE THE MEN'S AUXILIARY OF SCUM, THESE BENIGN MALES...

Or maybe because I got a bit drunk.

THESE ARE FROM THE MENS AUXILIARY OF SCUM.

What else was there to do?

# Friday, July twentieth

James Romberger asked me to do an interview by email for Publisher's Weekly. I said I'd rather do it in person, so we met at a cafe, but it turned out to be too loud there.

TESTING, TESTING...

We went to the back garden, where it was quiet, but it was 100 degrees outside.

WHERE DOES THE INFLUENCE OF THE BLACK SPOT SHADING COME FROM?

It began to rain.

TELL ME ABOUT YOUR APPROACH WITH THE "UNRELIABLE NARRATOR"..

It began to thunderstorm.

We sat there for a long time, watching the torrent.

ONCE I WAS ON A BUS AND I SAW A BOLT OF LIGHTNING HIT A STONE IN THE ROAD AND RICOCHET INTO A TREE, THEN A COW UNDERNEATH IT FELL DOWN DEAD AND A BIRD FELL OUT OF THE TREE ONTO IT.

Then we realized the recorder wasn't recording.

SORRY. I'M USED TO EMAIL INTERVIEWS.

YES. EMAIL ME YOUR QUESTIONS AND I'LL ANSWER THEM IN DEPTH.

## Saturday, July twenty-first

There's been a lot of activity at home lately. There's Sadie and lil' Chub-Chub, and Jenni's been crashing on the couch, and Tony stops by like Kramer. It's great except I'm always working.

THERE WAS A SUSHI PARTY! BUT NO ONE WAS EATING THE SUSHI SO IT BECAME A DANCE PARTY!

AW, MAN! I'D HAVE TOTALLY GONE TO THAT IF I DIDN'T HAVE TO DRAW THIS DUMB COMIC!

GABRIELLE, NO ONE IS MAKING YOU DO THAT! IT'S ONLY YOU!

To tell the truth, I haven't been doing so well lately. When I get all stressed out, I tend to obsess over some imaginary problem, to "catastrophize."

WHAT D'YOU THINK?

DOES IT ITCH?

NO, BUT WHAT IF IT'S SOME NEW STRAIN OF BEDBUG WHOSE BITES DON'T ITCH?

GABRIELLE, THAT'S A PIMPLE.

To stay focused, I've been listening to Patti Smith narrate her audiobook <u>Just Kids</u>, about her early days before becoming a rock star. How did she have time to live in the Chelsea Hotel with Robert Mapplethorpe, work full time, do her drawings and poetry and hang out at cafes with Allen Ginsberg and William Burroughs talking about Rimbaud and Jean Genet when I can't even manage to keep up with my emails?

And I can't help thinking, if I'd lived at the Chelsea Hotel, how it'd have been wasted on me.

HEYA GABRIELLE! HOW'S THE DRAWLIN' GOIN? WANNA COME HANG OUT WITH JANIS JOPLIN AN' ME?

I CAN'T! I PROMISED MYSELF I'D DO A COMIC EVERY DAY!

I had to get out of the house, to escape. So I packed up my art supplies (and there are a lot) to go stay at Steve's for the weekend.

DIARY

PAPER

LIGHT BOX

LIL IDEA BOOK

WACOM PEN

COMPUTER

FOUNTAIN & RAPIDOGRAPH PENS

WACOM TABLET

INK

SYRINGE (FOR INK)

But first I needed to make sure I didn't have bedbugs.

## Sunday, July Twenty-second

Steve lives way out on the other side of Brooklyn in an apartment over-looking Ocean Parkway, with its endless flow of commuters like a great big river leading to the sea.

Cherries are a good gift to bring, right? How do I know if these are good cherries or bad ones? I'll just buy 'em and worry about it later.

SALE! CHERRIES

These cherries are no good! They're soft and overripe. He'll think I got them on sale! He'll think I can't pick out cherries!

Wait... what is this?

CHERRIES

Ooh, these are much nicer! And I can pick out the firmest, deepest red, most perfect, juiciest ones! I will hand-select an entire bag of the choicest cherries.

I BROUGHT YOU A BAG OF BAD CHERRIES AND A BAG OF GOOD CHERRIES.

BUT YOU CAN'T HAVE EITHER JUST YET.

Here it is, my friends, a pie.

FLOUR

# Thursday, July twenty-sixth

It turns out the Bronx Zoo is very expensive, but on Wednesdays it's a free-for-all.

I THINK THE BEARS ARE THAT WAY.

WE HAVE TO WAIT FOR STEVE FOR THE BEARS!

The giraffes, awkward, weird, slow-moving, as if they were in another state of time, or on some sort of pharmaceutical drug.

The depressed polar bear, giving up in the ninety degree heat.

The emasculated grizzly.

The baboons.

And all those children.

# Friday, July twenty-seventh

Wandering through a deserted city, with only a bear for company, looking for something to eat.

Even a bear cannot protect you from zombies but it is a comfort to have around.

I found Boris when he was just a cub, recently escaped with his mother from the Bronx zoo, after she unwittingly rescued me from zombies.

A bear will only attack you if it is startled, to protect its cubs or if it is starving. I read that somewhere.

One day we came to an abandoned house, where in the attic we found a baby, malnourished but alive.

By morning the baby was eaten, and I knew it was only a matter of time before I was next. There is a reason that bears and people cannot be friends.

But as soon as I left, I regretted it. I wasn't sure what I felt more sharply: my hunger, my fear or my loneliness. And so I concluded I had nothing left to live for. I determined the best thing to do was to find some zombies and just let them have at me.

And then one day, I ran into my friend Sadie!

SADIE!?

She didn't seem to recognize me! Was she a zombie? If so, why wouldn't she eat me? Was it some deeply buried loyalty, unmarred even by undeath?

I DON'T CARE! COME BACK AND EAT ME!

I DON'T WANNA LIVE ANYWAY!

I followed her. She was inhumanly strong and fast.

She scaled a building and slipped through a little window.

I searched the building up and down but it was totally abandoned.

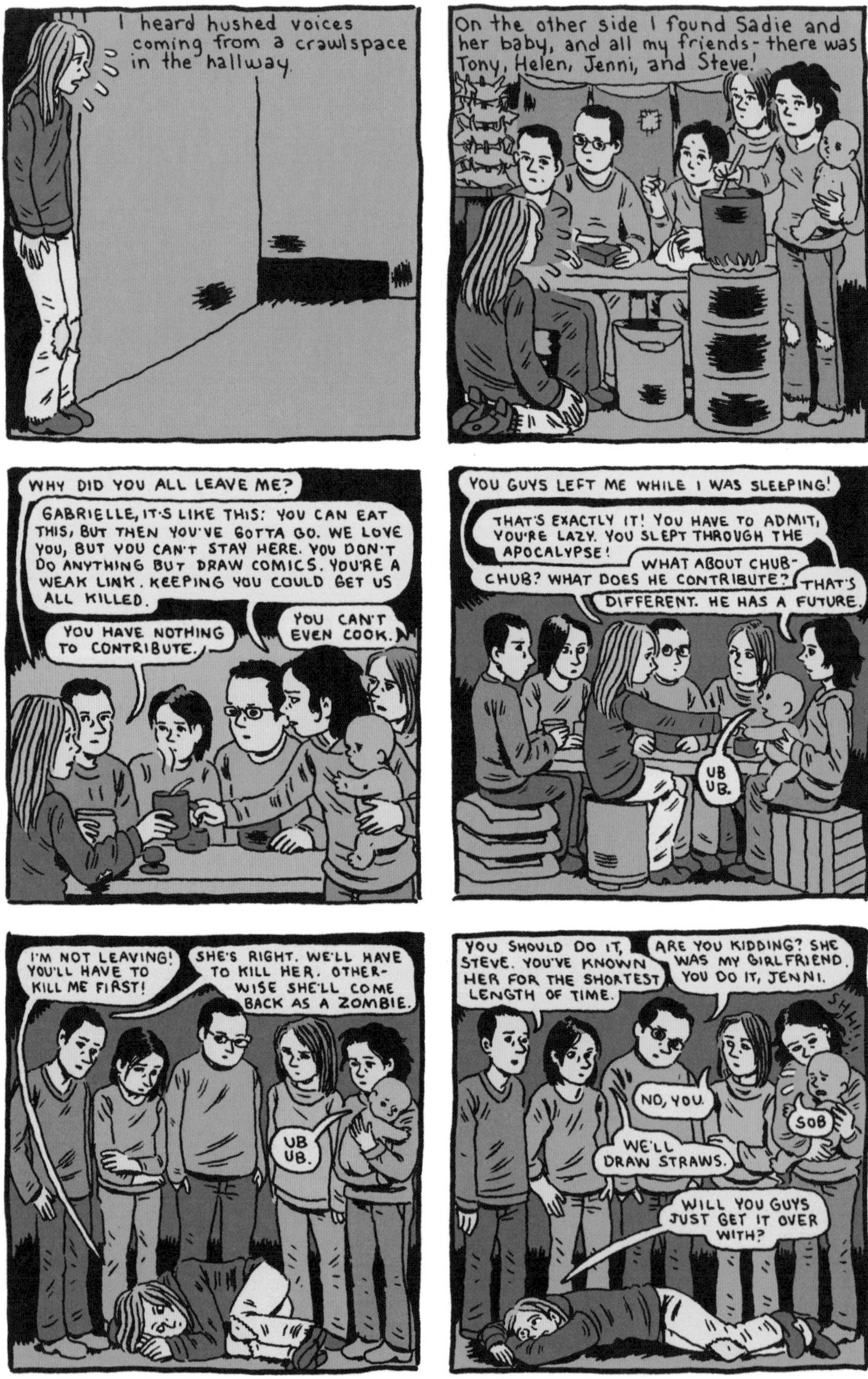

I heard hushed voices coming from a crawlspace in the hallway.
On the other side I found Sadie and her baby, and all my friends - there was Tony, Helen, Jenni, and Steve!
WHY DID YOU ALL LEAVE ME?
GABRIELLE, IT'S LIKE THIS: YOU CAN EAT THIS, BUT THEN YOU'VE GOTTA GO. WE LOVE YOU, BUT YOU CAN'T STAY HERE. YOU DON'T DO ANYTHING BUT DRAW COMICS. YOU'RE A WEAK LINK. KEEPING YOU COULD GET US ALL KILLED.
YOU HAVE NOTHING TO CONTRIBUTE.
YOU CAN'T EVEN COOK.
YOU GUYS LEFT ME WHILE I WAS SLEEPING!
THAT'S EXACTLY IT! YOU HAVE TO ADMIT, YOU'RE LAZY. YOU SLEPT THROUGH THE APOCALYPSE!
WHAT ABOUT CHUB-CHUB? WHAT DOES HE CONTRIBUTE?
THAT'S DIFFERENT. HE HAS A FUTURE.
UB UB.
I'M NOT LEAVING! YOU'LL HAVE TO KILL ME FIRST!
SHE'S RIGHT. WE'LL HAVE TO KILL HER. OTHER-WISE SHE'LL COME BACK AS A ZOMBIE.
UB UB.
YOU SHOULD DO IT, STEVE. YOU'VE KNOWN HER FOR THE SHORTEST LENGTH OF TIME.
ARE YOU KIDDING? SHE WAS MY GIRLFRIEND. YOU DO IT, JENNI.
SHH!
NO, YOU.
SOB
WE'LL DRAW STRAWS.
WILL YOU GUYS JUST GET IT OVER WITH?

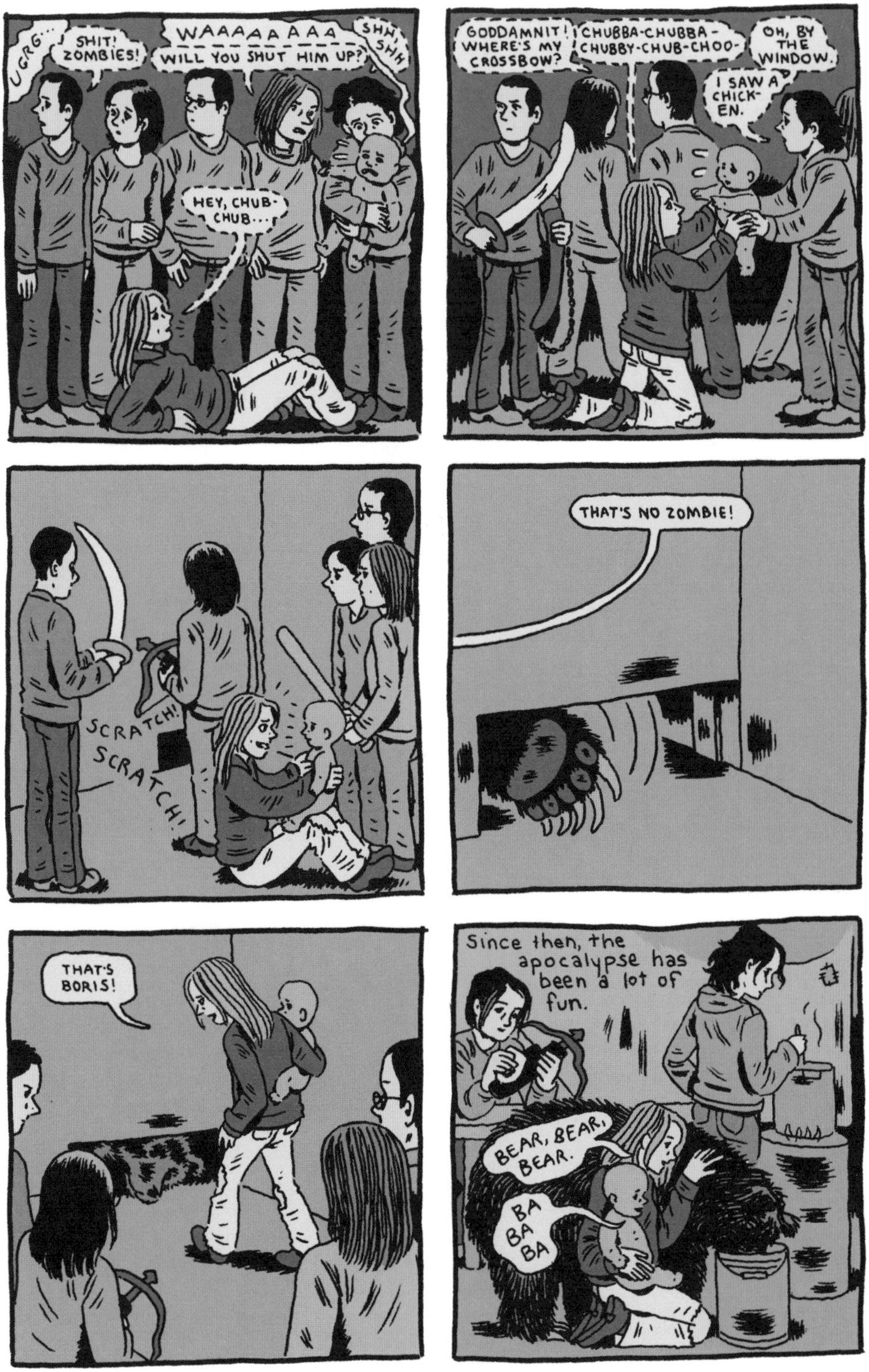
UGRG...
SHIT! ZOMBIES!
WAAAAAAAA
WILL YOU SHUT HIM UP?
SHH, SHH
HEY, CHUB-CHUB...
GODDAMNIT! WHERE'S MY CROSSBOW?
CHUBBA-CHUBBA-CHUBBY-CHUB-CHOO-
OH, BY THE WINDOW.
I SAW A CHICK-EN.
SCRATCH!
SCRATCH!
THAT'S NO ZOMBIE!
THAT'S BORIS!
Since then, the apocalypse has been a lot of fun.
BEAR, BEAR, BEAR.
BA BA BA

# Monday, July thirteeth

**Panel 1:**

Oh no! It's nine o'clock at night and I haven't even thought of a comic!

YOU ARE DOING THIS TO YOURSELF. NO ONE IS MAKING YOU DO IT.

**Panel 2:**

For the first two weeks of this, it was easy. I was living my life and turning it into art. Or at least comics.

NO, I'M NOT! THIS IS MY WORK! JUST LIKE YOUR WORK IS YOURS.

**Panel 3:**

But then something in my head dried up and it felt like there was a dark cloud over my head all the time, pressing on me.

THERE, THERE, BABY, SHHH... SHH

WAAAAAH

THIS IS SO HARD. I DUNNO WHAT TO DO.

**Panel 4:**

In Just Kids, Sam Shepard & Patti Smith made it look easy when they were writing a play.

WHAT IF I MESS UP? WHAT IF I SCREW UP THE RHYTHM?

YOU CAN'T MAKE A MISTAKE WHEN YOU'RE IMPROVISING!

IT'S LIKE DRUMMING-IF YOU MISS A BEAT, YOU CREATE ANOTHER.

**Panel 5:**

Oh no! It's midnight Now! I've got nothing! Guess I'll write my autobiography: After a troubled childhood, I enrolled in college, then promptly dropped out to spend my life drawing comics.

**Panel 6:**

My education came from giving up-on school, on my ideas of normal, and of art and success. But to give up, one has to try in the first place.

We went to see the Monica Bill Barnes Dance Company. They dance as if they can't dance. They're masters of obstructions and false starts. They make blunders on purpose. They give themselves flowers.

I wanted to bring Sadie to see them, but she had that dumb old baby. I can't believe Sadie's a single mom and a pilot.

I first met Sadie while standing next to her in an alphabetically-ordered line. Her name was Hales and mine was Hayes (my mother's maiden name).

When we were older, we traveled all over the world together. We'd spend hours just walking, not speaking. Once as we were walking in a forest, the path took two different directions. Without conferring with each other, we went separate ways.

As I walked alone I thought, 'this is good, we'll each have the benefit of each others' experience.'

What's that? I'm done here? Oh, for me? Why, thank you! Oh my god! I don't know what to say! I love you all!!!

105

Oslo Comics Expo, Oslo, Norway,
June 7th-8th, 2013

June 4th 2013

Hey, I'm at the airport! I'm going to Oslo!

CAN I HAVE A MEDIUM STRAWBERRY EXTREME?

OKAY THANKS I LOVE YOU TOO BYE.

For an impoverished cartoonist, I do an awful lot of international traveling. I remember wandering around so many airports, looking for someplace to plug in my computer, or my phone, or for something reasonable to eat, feeling generally uncomfortable, that they all blur into each other.

After awhile, the novelty is no longer- oh look, somebody left a nearly untouched grandé caramel frappuccino behind! Even the whipped cream is mostly intact!

Ugh. I am instantly punished with illness and a chill. I want to throw up and roll up in a blanket.

and stop judging me! I'm suffering enough!

Maybe I am one of those people who are afflicted with too much consciousness.

Do these people have a problem with consciousness?

OF ALL THE PHOTOS I POSTED THE ONLY ONE SHE "LIKES" IS THAT ONE!

CHELSEA "LIKED" YOUR POST.

CHELSEA AND I BOTH POSTED THE SAME PICTURE AND HAD A LIKING COMPETITION. I GOT MORE LIKES BUT SHE GOT MORE COMMENTS.

A COMMENT IS LIKE FOUR LIKES.

On the plane I had some sort of attack of the nerves. I started by regretting every choice I've ever made, and continued by preemptively regretting every choice I will make, because I'm inevitably poised to choose the wrong ones.

And it wasn't the fear of flying either. In fact I wished the plane would dive straight into the ground and extinguish us all like a cigarette butt, putting an end to this slow motion train wreck of a life.

On a layover in Reykjavik, I figured it was as good a time as any to try the Xanax my psychiatrist prescribed. Suddenly, I was struck by a great sense of connection. Here we all were, at the airport, on a great adventure together! I felt like speaking to everybody, these brothers and sisters of mine.

THERE'S ANOTHER RESTROOM RIGHT DOWN THIS HALL THAT'S TOTALLY EMPTY.

Flu Hartberg picked Michael Deforge and me up from the airport. As we passed the dazzling countryside by train, Flu told us about the moose who sometimes visit his back yard.

ARE THEY DANGEROUS?

NO! UNLESS YOU GET BETWEEN THEM AND THEIR YOUNG.

LIKE BEARS.

YES, WE HAVE BEARS, TOO.

POLAR BEARS?

THE POLAR BEARS ARE FAR IN THE NORTH OF NORWAY, IN THE SVALBARD ISLANDS. PEOPLE WHO LIVE THERE HAVE TO CARRY GUNS IN CASE THEY RUN INTO ONE.

I got my very own swank two bedroom apartment, designed in the theme of the home of a successful yet loveless woman in her thirties waiting for her heart to be melted by some rugged troublemaker.

After a nice long nap I had fourteen dollar beers (Oslo is possibly the most expensive city in the world!) with Michael Deforge. We only just met, but we're both cartoonists.

I SHOULD GO BACK SOON AND GET A BIT MORE WORK DONE TONIGHT, OTHERWISE I'LL HATE MYSELF.

I HATE MYSELF.

June 5th

I carefully studied the map, because I know I've got a propensity for getting lost. Nonetheless, I immediately got lost. These buildings and streets would not correspond with the lines on paper.

No choice but to humiliate myself.

EXCUSE ME. DO YOU SPEAK ENGLISH?

YES?

DO YOU KNOW HOW TO FIND CENTRAL STATION?

YES, IT'S ABOUT FIFTY MINUTES FROM HERE.

JUST KIDDING, IT'S RIGHT THERE.

I waited for a very long time for the Frognerseteren train and then for no reason I can think of got on the wrong train.

I jumped off and hopped on the train back to Central Station and resumed my wait for the Frognerseteren-bound train.

Fifteen minutes later I realized I had to go across again, back to where I'd started.

But no, it turned out I'd been originally wrong.

FROGNERSETEREN

The next train wouldn't come for another twenty minutes. I sat down and wept, not for the time lost but for the unreliability of my own mind.

What was I thinking about, that was so distracting? I was making up stories in my head, and they were riveting.

I SEEN YOU STARING AT MY DOG. YOU WANT HIM? TAKE HIM. HERE, TAKE THE KEYS TO MY HOUSE, AND MY CAR, I'M DONE WITH THIS LIFE.

I rode all the way out to the end of the line.

I hiked through the mountains. I was hoping to see a moose.

If I'm gonna have a chance to see a moose I should get off the beaten path.

And I should learn not to tromp so loudly, but to creep.

There was a little lodge out there where you could buy a waffle and a hot chocolate. They don't have places like these in America. And that's where I got to see a moose.

It's funny how a thing like a moose can come into your consciousness. I never even thought about one before, except in cartoons. It's like a deer, but bigger and goofier.

June 6th Ladies & gentlemen: Scott McCloud, Gabrielle Bell & Michael Deforge!

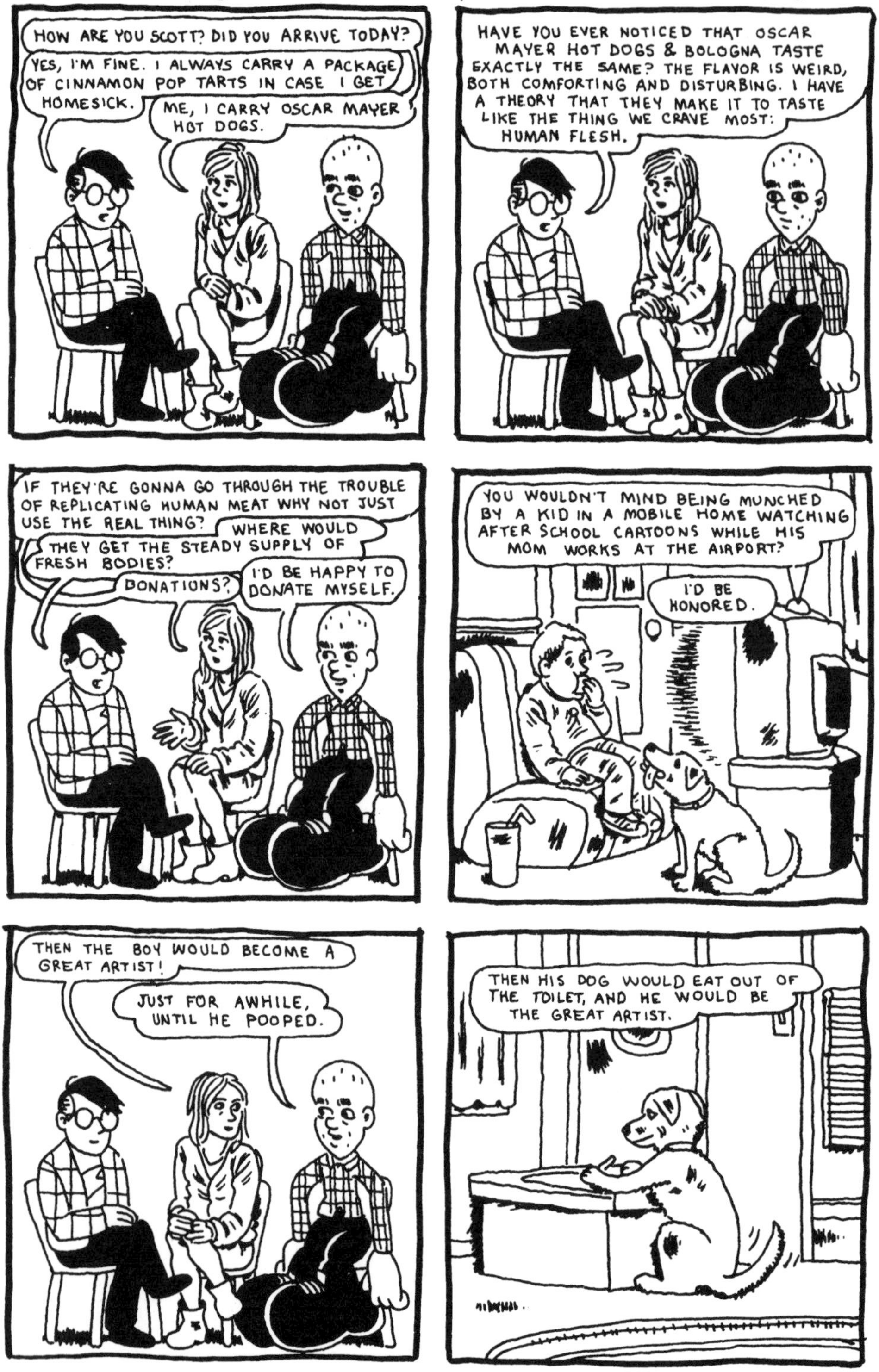
HOW ARE YOU SCOTT? DID YOU ARRIVE TODAY?
YES, I'M FINE. I ALWAYS CARRY A PACKAGE OF CINNAMON POP TARTS IN CASE I GET HOMESICK.
ME, I CARRY OSCAR MAYER HOT DOGS.
HAVE YOU EVER NOTICED THAT OSCAR MAYER HOT DOGS & BOLOGNA TASTE EXACTLY THE SAME? THE FLAVOR IS WEIRD, BOTH COMFORTING AND DISTURBING. I HAVE A THEORY THAT THEY MAKE IT TO TASTE LIKE THE THING WE CRAVE MOST: HUMAN FLESH.
IF THEY'RE GONNA GO THROUGH THE TROUBLE OF REPLICATING HUMAN MEAT WHY NOT JUST USE THE REAL THING?
WHERE WOULD THEY GET THE STEADY SUPPLY OF FRESH BODIES?
DONATIONS?
I'D BE HAPPY TO DONATE MYSELF.
YOU WOULDN'T MIND BEING MUNCHED BY A KID IN A MOBILE HOME WATCHING AFTER SCHOOL CARTOONS WHILE HIS MOM WORKS AT THE AIRPORT?
I'D BE HONORED.
THEN THE BOY WOULD BECOME A GREAT ARTIST!
JUST FOR AWHILE, UNTIL HE POOPED.
THEN HIS DOG WOULD EAT OUT OF THE TOILET, AND HE WOULD BE THE GREAT ARTIST.

June 8th

On Saturday I had some onstage interviews. But first I had to introduce myself.

HI. I'M GABRIELLE...I DO AUTOBIOGRAPHICAL COMICS... AND THAT'S ABOUT IT...

Never fear, I remembered, Xanax is here! Soon I was taking on twentieth-century American literature.

"THINLY DISGUISED" AUTOBIOGRAPHY ONLY ADDS A LAYER OF FALSITY TO THE WORK. LIKE IN ON THE ROAD. YOU'RE JUST TRYING TO FIGURE OUT WHICH ONE'S NEAL CASSADY, WHO'S ALLEN GINSBERG. JUST USE REAL NAMES!

AND ZUCKERMAN UNBOUND? I'VE SEEN THAT PHILIP ROTH DOCUMENTARY! STOP BEING COY!

Also, Norwegian literature.

AND WHAT ABOUT THIS MIN KAMP, WITH ITS SOMBER, ABSTRACT PAINTING ON THE COVER, PROCLAIMING: "THIS IS IMPORTANT SELF-REVELATION!" IF A WOMAN HAD WRITTEN THAT, THEY'D HAVE BEEN ALL, "WHO DOES SHE THINK SHE IS?!"

Later I was glad to know I wasn't the only one stymied by the Oslo streets when Michael and I tried to find a club called Blå, to see a friend from New York play, just a block from our apartment.

WASN'T IT JUST PAST THE BRIDGE ON NORDRE GATE?

I THOUGHT IT WAS JUST BEFORE THE BRIDGE ON NEDRE GATE.

I THOUGHT IT WAS THE SAME THING.

Asking was no help this time.

EXCUSE ME...UH...DO YOU KNOW WHERE A CLUB CALLED...UH... BLAHR IS?

I DON'T KNOW, I DON'T CARE, HELL, SHIT, FUCK OFF.

OKAY. WELL, THANKS ANYWAY!

So a bunch of us went to the roof of our building and watched it never get dark.

July 2013

Monday, July first, 2013

I'm on my porch! Well, it's not technically mine. I'm renting an apartment in an old Victorian house. This is my writer's residency, because I can't get it together to apply for, let alone be accepted to one.

I am pretty happy out here, but at night it gets so quiet I start to worry about a sex-crazed maniac breaking in to rape and kill me.

SMASH!

When that doesn't happen, I worry that this house is haunted.

OH, GREAT! NOW THAT I'VE THOUGHT OF THEM, I'VE SUMMONED GHOSTS!

Everywhere in this town, lawns are being mowed, and there is the constant smell of fresh-cut grass.

It'd be lovely if I hadn't learned on NPR that the odor is from the panic hormones released upon imminent decapitation.

That is why I don't listen to NPR anymore. I still enjoy the flowers. Don't tell me about the flowers.

Tuesday, July second

Tony gave me a lift to the train station. But first I stopped in to see Gabe at Desert Island.

I missed the train so I went to visit Larry and wait for the next one.

Since we had some extra time we stopped in at Adam Baumgold's gallery to see Charles Burns' portraits.

Then to Art Brown for ink since it was nearby.

Every single interaction is painful. I never get used to it. I never develop calluses. It just chafes. How do you people manage it?

Out here, I can go for days without any interactions, except for the occasional

# Wednesday, July third

Dear Steven,
I know this might be terribly inconvenient, so don't worry if you can't, but near the train station is Art Brown, the only place that sells the kind of ink I use. Can you possibly stop and pick a bottle up for me on your way here? If you're coming by car or if you can't for whatever reason don't worry, I'll make do.

OH PLEASE LET HIM GET THE INK OR I AM SCREWED...

In fact Steve was going to drive, but first he took the hour-long subway ride up to midtown to get my ink.

DO YOU HAVE THIS ONE IN BLACK?

NO.

WHEN—

MAYBE NEXT WEEK.

He did some research and learned that the ink could be found at a store downtown, so he hopped on the 6 train and that's where he went.

SALE

He waited for an A train that never came so had to take a detour uptown where he missed three overcrowded F trains. He was dizzy because it was ninety degrees and he'd forgotten to eat.

Meanwhile, I realized I'd been wearing the same dress for five days and it smelled nasty. I spent the afternoon deciding which outfit to wear for the next five days.

When Steve got home, instead of getting in his car, he turned on the air conditioner, turned off the lights and went back to bed.

## Thursday, July fourth

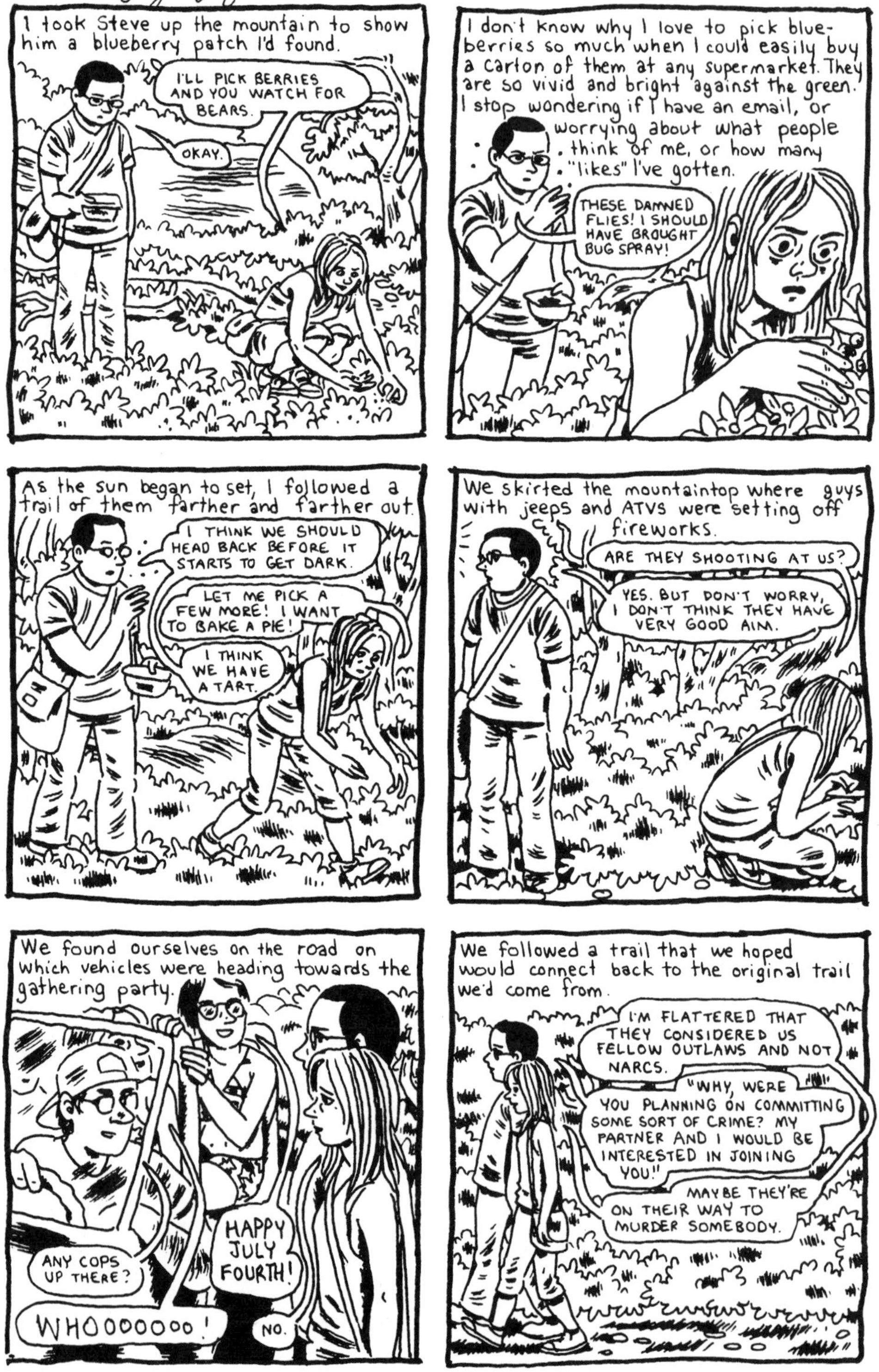
I took Steve up the mountain to show him a blueberry patch I'd found.
I'LL PICK BERRIES AND YOU WATCH FOR BEARS.
OKAY.
I don't know why I love to pick blueberries so much when I could easily buy a carton of them at any supermarket. They are so vivid and bright against the green. I stop wondering if I have an email, or worrying about what people think of me, or how many "likes" I've gotten.
THESE DAMNED FLIES! I SHOULD HAVE BROUGHT BUG SPRAY!
As the sun began to set, I followed a trail of them farther and farther out.
I THINK WE SHOULD HEAD BACK BEFORE IT STARTS TO GET DARK.
LET ME PICK A FEW MORE! I WANT TO BAKE A PIE!
I THINK WE HAVE A TART.
We skirted the mountaintop where guys with jeeps and ATVS were setting off fireworks.
ARE THEY SHOOTING AT US?
YES. BUT DON'T WORRY, I DON'T THINK THEY HAVE VERY GOOD AIM.
We found ourselves on the road on which vehicles were heading towards the gathering party.
ANY COPS UP THERE?
HAPPY JULY FOURTH!
WHOOOOOOO!
NO.
We followed a trail that we hoped would connect back to the original trail we'd come from.
I'M FLATTERED THAT THEY CONSIDERED US FELLOW OUTLAWS AND NOT NARCS.
"WHY, WERE YOU PLANNING ON COMMITTING SOME SORT OF CRIME? MY PARTNER AND I WOULD BE INTERESTED IN JOINING YOU!"
MAYBE THEY'RE ON THEIR WAY TO MURDER SOMEBODY.

We walked and walked and walked.

WE SHOULD TURN BACK. I DON'T THINK WE'RE GOING IN THE RIGHT DIRECTION.

BUT MAYBE THERE'S SOMETHING JUST AROUND THIS NEXT CORNER.

OKAY. ONE MORE CORNER.

I SMELL A CAMPFIRE! WE SHOULD FOLLOW IT AND ASK FOR DIRECTIONS!

WE DON'T NEED DIRECTIONS. I KNOW HOW TO GET BACK.

OR MAYBE YOU'RE AFRAID?

I'M NOT AFRAID! WE JUST HAVE TO RETRACE OUR FOOTSTEPS BACK.

THESE DAMNED FLIES!

BUT YOU WERE THE ONE WHO SAID WE SHOULD TAKE THIS TRAIL!

CAN WE PLEASE NOT ARGUE? IT'S GETTING LATE.

I'M SORRY BUT

CAN YOU STOP? I CAN'T SEE WELL AND I NEED TO FOCUS ON THE TRAIL.

I WASN'T

STOP!

BUT I WASN'T

STEVE!

SLIP!!

I'M OKAY. JUST PLEASE LET'S NOT ARGUE.

ALL RIGHT. I'LL STAY IN FRONT AND WATCH FOR OBSTACLES.

ROCK!

ROCK.

ROCK.

ROCK.

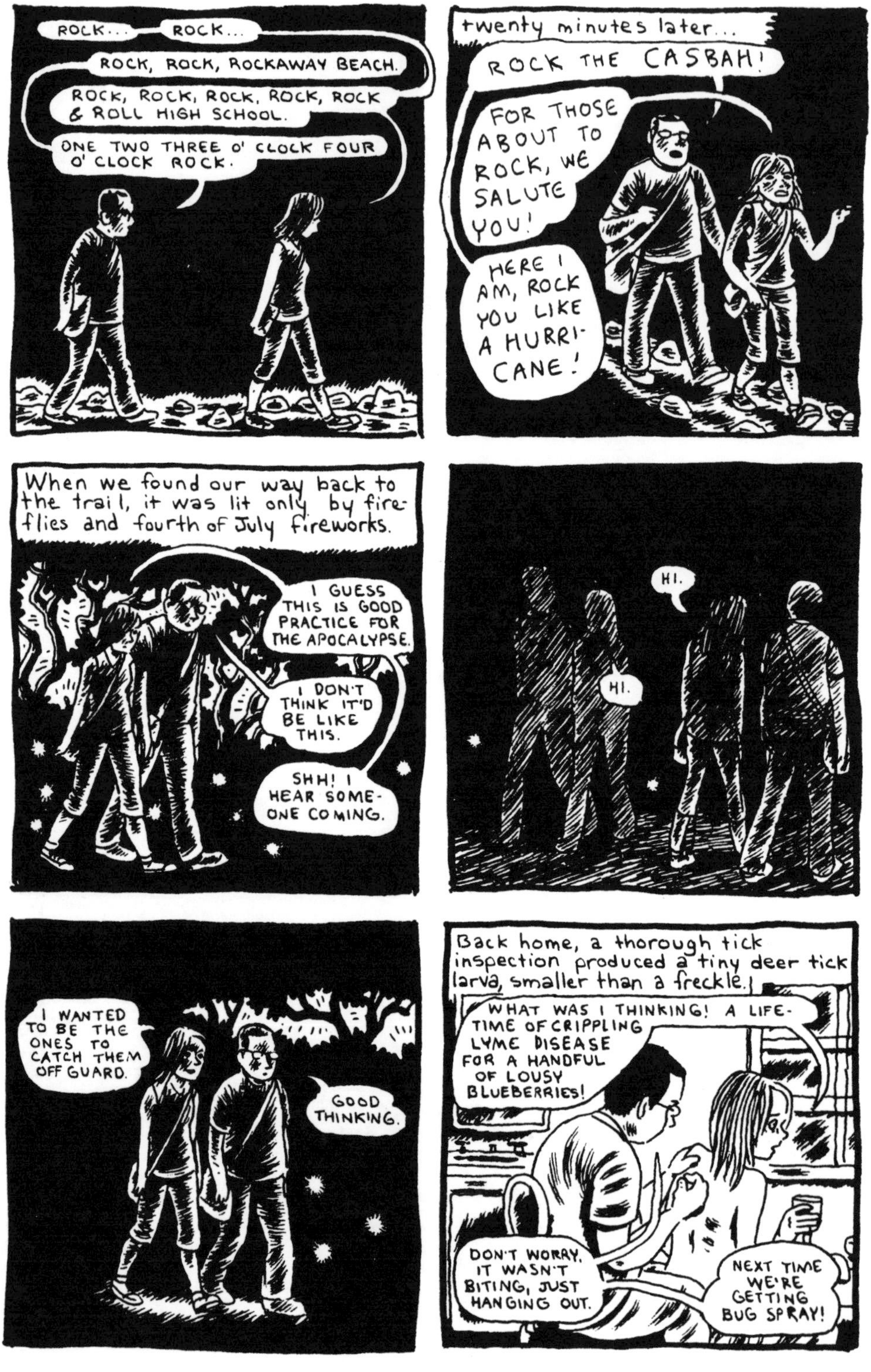
ROCK...
ROCK...
ROCK, ROCK, ROCKAWAY BEACH.
ROCK, ROCK, ROCK, ROCK, ROCK & ROLL HIGH SCHOOL.
ONE TWO THREE O' CLOCK FOUR O' CLOCK ROCK.
twenty minutes later...
ROCK THE CASBAH!
FOR THOSE ABOUT TO ROCK, WE SALUTE YOU!
HERE I AM, ROCK YOU LIKE A HURRICANE!
When we found our way back to the trail, it was lit only by fireflies and fourth of July fireworks.
I GUESS THIS IS GOOD PRACTICE FOR THE APOCALYPSE.
I DON'T THINK IT'D BE LIKE THIS.
SHH! I HEAR SOMEONE COMING.
HI.
HI.
I WANTED TO BE THE ONES TO CATCH THEM OFF GUARD.
GOOD THINKING.
Back home, a thorough tick inspection produced a tiny deer tick larva, smaller than a freckle.
WHAT WAS I THINKING! A LIFETIME OF CRIPPLING LYME DISEASE FOR A HANDFUL OF LOUSY BLUEBERRIES!
DON'T WORRY, IT WASN'T BITING, JUST HANGING OUT.
NEXT TIME WE'RE GETTING BUG SPRAY!

## Sunday, July seventh

I walk to the library to use the internet with all the other kooks.

In fact, this town is full of kooks, but they're not mean about it.

THAT GIRL TOOK MY SPOT.

THAT'S TOO BAD.

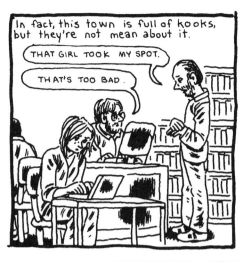

In fact, they're the only people I ever speak to around here.

EXCUSE ME, DO EITHER OF YOU KNOW WHICH OF THESE COLORS WOULD SUIT MY SKIN BETTER?

I JUST USE POWDER.

I have a fantasy of moving far away, miles out in the wilderness, and never leaving. Every few weeks I'd have a friend deliver supplies. I'd make them dinner with vegetables from my garden, and that would be all the society I'd need.

Come to think of it, that dream is a slightly idealized version of my mom's life, the same one I desperately dreamed of escaping since I was small.

My mom is the ultimate kook. I used to be mortified with embarrassment by her. Now I'm proud of her, and proud of myself for even owning a computer.

THERE'S PICTURES OF YOU AND YOUR BROTHERS ON THERE?

YES, HUNDREDS OF THEM! AND THEY'RE ALL CHRONOLOGICALLY ARRANGED, WITH LABELS THAT TELL YOU WHO THEY'RE WITH AND WHERE THEY ARE.

## Monday, July eighth

I wonder how long it'd take, by just sitting here, for my mind to become still, the way a muddy pool slowly clears until you see through to the ground. And by sitting I mean drawing, writing, reading, thinking, eating fruit and vegetables and dancing around in my underwear.

But I got a text from Tony, who was passing through on his way to Massachusetts with some things to drop off for me. So in honor of his visit I vacuumed, though I liked how the carpet looked like a forest floor.

Tony brought me my scanner, a TV/DVD player, some tools and a coat rack. Also he's been trying to give me an extra toaster he owns, because he cannot stand for objects to go ownerless.

I DON'T WANT A BUNCH OF STUFF HERE! IF I WANT TOAST I'LL MAKE IT IN THE BROILER.

BUT COOKING GAS IS MORE EXPENSIVE THAN ELECTRICITY.

MY COOKING GAS IS INCLUDED IN THE RENT.

ARE YOU SURE? LET ME SEE YOUR LEASE.

He also brought his leftover New Yorkers which I read while he fussed around.

DID YOU SEE THAT ARTICLE ABOUT LYME DISEASE?

I'M READING IT NOW.

Eventually I thought I'd better get some work done.

THIS ISN'T COMING OUT SO GOOD. I WONDER IF I SHOULD LEAVE THIS PART FOR TOMORROW MORNING WHEN MY MIND'S SHARPER.

THAT SOUNDS LIKE A GOOD IDEA.

THEN AGAIN, I DON'T WANT TO SET THAT KIND OF PRECEDENT.

THAT'S TRUE.

WAIT A MINUTE...

WHEN DID I GET A HUSBAND?!

Tuesday, July ninth

The trouble with me is that I swing between exhaustion and antsiness, with no middle ground. Take yesterday, for example. I sat down to work and discovered I had an ant on me!

Also I couldn't sit still, so I biked to the mountain, climbed to the top and picked blueberries and flowers.

I HOPE A BEAR DOESN'T SNEAK UP AND ATTACK ME.

HOPE I DON'T GET LYME DISEASE.

I HOPE A RANGER DOESN'T COME UP AND ARREST ME.

When I got back I was exhausted.

So I went out for coffee. And for good measure, I went out for ice cream.

ARE YOU READY?

SORRY BUT THIS IS A VERY IMPORTANT DECISION.

Then: antsy. So I hiked over to the drug store to buy a Brita.

DO YOU SELL BRITAS?

NO.

IS THERE ANYWHERE AROUND HERE WHERE I COULD GET ONE?

NO.

IS IT BECAUSE THE TAP WATER IS SO FRESH AND CLEAN IN THIS TOWN A BRITA ISN'T NEEDED?

NO.

I bought a three gallon container of water and carried it home, stopping every ten feet or so to rest.

## Wednesday, July tenth

Maybe I should try to make a friend. I've heard that, if you go to summer camp, if you can make just one friend, you're good. I don't particularly want a friend, though I suppose one would be useful to learn things from, like whether the tap water here is potable.

But who needs a friend when you've got the internet?!

No, seriously though. I have friends! Like for example, my good friend Aaron (Renier) called me just last night.

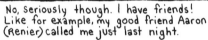

AARON! I HAVEN'T HEARD FROM YOU SINCE FEBRUARY! I THOUGHT YOU WERE MAD AT ME. I WAS GONNA WRITE YOU AN EMAIL. BUT I DIDN'T.

OF COURSE I'M NOT MAD AT YOU! I'M JUST FLAKY!

Aaron told me about how his neighbor Laura (Park) along with his girlfriend Jessica (Campbell) asked him to help figure out what to do about this dog with enormous testicles that showed up on Laura's porch.

I'VE GOT WORK TO DO!

YOU SHOULD KEEP HIM!

NO WAY! BUT HE NEEDS A BATH!

Just to extricate himself, he took the dog back to his apartment and gave it a bath.

He bought it a leash and a collar. The woman at the pet shop said the dog looked familiar. She suggested he try walking it around the neighborhood to see if it'd recognize its home. It didn't.

He took it to the vet to find out if it had a microchip implant, and they told him the dog had cancer.

He decided to bring it to a no-kill shelter, but for that he had to get it neutered. When he took the dog back to the vet they told him it wasn't cancer after all, it was a hernia leaking guts into its scrotum.

YOU JUST DON'T WANT TO KEEP HIM BECAUSE OF HIS BIG OL' NUTSACK!

THAT'S NOT TRUE! I JUST DON'T WANT A DOG!

He wondered, who's going to adopt a five-year old mutt with a giant scrotum?

And then he realized that his mood was improved, he was walking in the park every day, and his relationship with Jessica was better.

And the dog seemed to love him.

Aaron named his dog Tanuki, after a Japanese raccoon dog mythologized for its enormous scrotum, believed to have magic powers.

# friday, July twelfth

Sadie drove up with her son Sylvester (formerly known as Chub-Chub) to visit. It seemed there would be no work done today.

I couldn't think of a comic anyway.

BUUUUUU BUUUUUUUUUH
BUUUUUUU UUH
BUUUUUUUH
BUUUUUUH

HE THINKS WE'RE BABBLING LIKE HIM!

I'm always standing on ceremony, waiting to be alone again.

LOOK, SYLVESTER! FIREFLIES!

At the end of the day I was considering having my tubes tied in a Gordian knot.

IT MUST GET PRETTY TIRING.

I'M USED TO IT NOW.

WAAAH AAAAAA AH

I am a beast, a savage, an animal that cowers in its cave.

I LOOK LIKE AN OLD CRONE TRYING TO EAT YOUR SON IN THESE PICTURES!

But at least I'm friends with these two.

Saturday, July thirteenth

Sadie gave me a lift back to the city, where she was staying with my sub-letter.

DON'T CHOKE ON THAT CARROT, OKAY?

First I went to see my friend Rachel. Rachel is very stylish. She is also very fascinated by me.

IN THE CITY PEOPLE DON'T HAVE TO BE NICE TO EACH OTHER. OUT THERE THEY HAVE TO AT LEAST PRETEND TO BE KIND BECAUSE THEY KNOW THEY'LL SEE EACH OTHER AGAIN.

Oh, who am I kidding. I only wish she was my friend. But then she wouldn't be my therapist.

I WANT TO BE ALONE ALL THE TIME. EVERY-BODY MAKES ME ANXIOUS. EVEN YOU. EITHER THAT OR THEY IRRITATE ME. WHATEVER THEY DO, THEY MAKE ME DIS-CONNECT WITH MYSELF.

But actually she's not my therapist any-more, either, because I was about to go back to my apartment and find a letter saying I'd been disqualified from Medicaid. I made too much money, but not enough to afford Rachel.

WE'RE OUT OF TIME BUT I'D LIKE TO EXPLORE THAT NEXT WEEK.

I've been neglecting things at home.

ARE YOU UPSET ABOUT THAT COMIC?

I DON'T READ YOUR COMICS.

IT'S JUST THAT I FELT LIKE I WAS BEGINNING TO FEEL A BIT HAPPY AND STABLE, BUT NOW IT'S GONE.

THERE'S NEVER ANY REST.

BUH BUH BUH BUH BUH BUH BUH BUH BUH

I KNOW THINGS ARE TOUGH ALL OVER. I MEAN, I'M TALKING TO A SINGLE MOM!

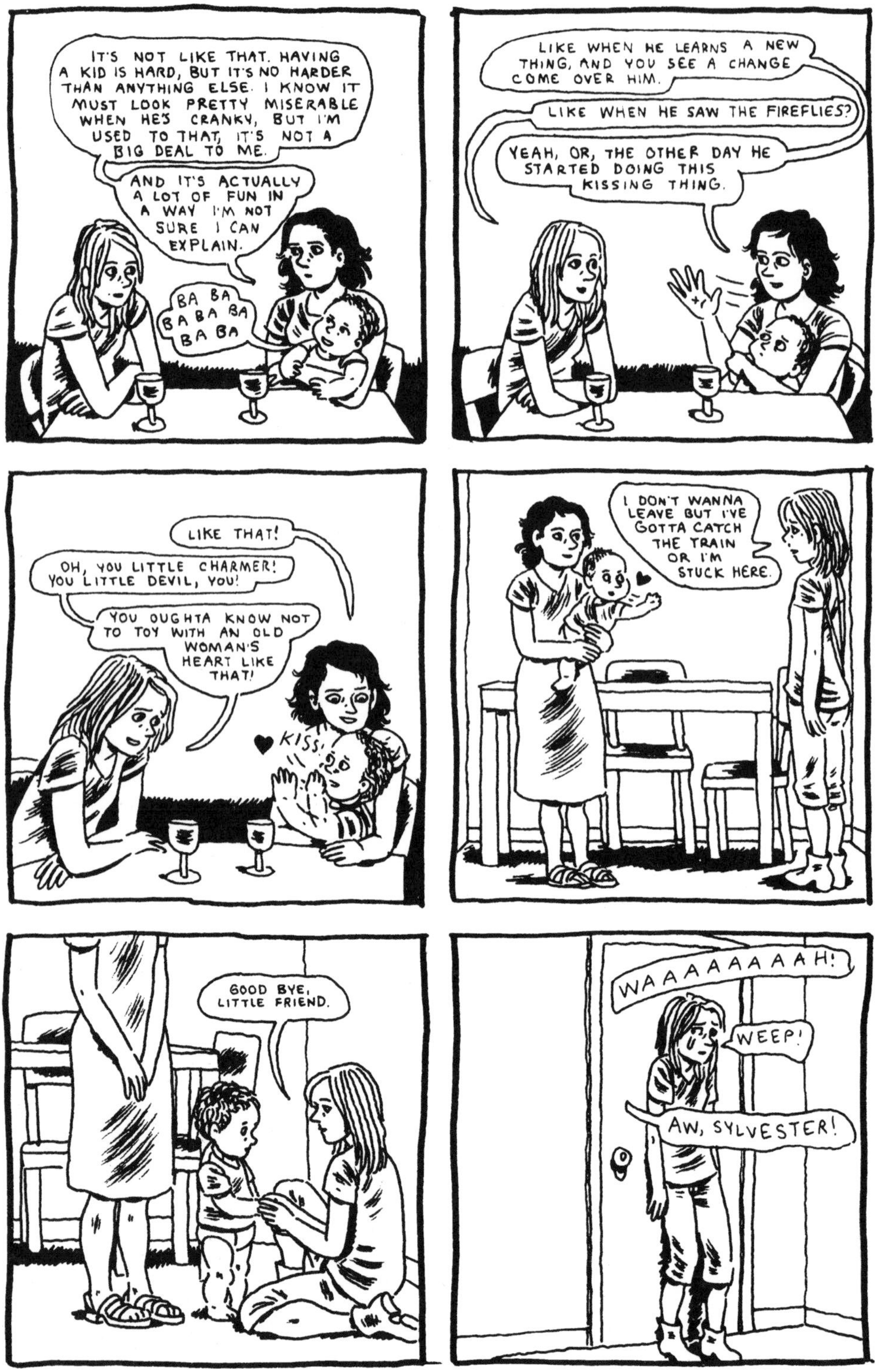
IT'S NOT LIKE THAT. HAVING A KID IS HARD, BUT IT'S NO HARDER THAN ANYTHING ELSE. I KNOW IT MUST LOOK PRETTY MISERABLE WHEN HE'S CRANKY, BUT I'M USED TO THAT, IT'S NOT A BIG DEAL TO ME.
AND IT'S ACTUALLY A LOT OF FUN IN A WAY I'M NOT SURE I CAN EXPLAIN.
BA BA BA BA BA BA BA
LIKE WHEN HE LEARNS A NEW THING, AND YOU SEE A CHANGE COME OVER HIM.
LIKE WHEN HE SAW THE FIREFLIES?
YEAH, OR, THE OTHER DAY HE STARTED DOING THIS KISSING THING.
LIKE THAT!
OH, YOU LITTLE CHARMER! YOU LITTLE DEVIL, YOU!
YOU OUGHTA KNOW NOT TO TOY WITH AN OLD WOMAN'S HEART LIKE THAT!
KISS!
I DON'T WANNA LEAVE BUT I'VE GOTTA CATCH THE TRAIN OR I'M STUCK HERE.
GOOD BYE, LITTLE FRIEND.
WAAAAAAAAH!
WEEP!
AW, SYLVESTER!

I believe I am done with other people.

It is true that when I spend time alone I grow even more awkward, more weird, more unapproachable, but if I choose not to associate with anyone, who is there to care?

People! They are so annoying, yammering away with their opinions and feelings and anecdotes and advice. I sit and wait for them to go away, and even after they do their voices continue to yammer in my head.

All the little things they say, they sting and bite and wear you down. I'd rather be eaten alive by insects.

"But you need other people, to challenge you, to show you other perspectives." I am a challenge enough to myself, and other people squash MY perspective. "But what about love?" I love myself, thank you! "What about for practical things, like help moving furniture?" Furniture is for other people! I will do without! "What about someone to argue with?" I am done arguing!

Other people tell me who I am supposed to be. Other people tell me what reality is. I don't want to know. I'm covered in bruises and scars. I'm going in here now. No, you can't come. Good bye!

# Tuesday, July sixteenth

What've I been reading, you ask? Well, I've been trying to get through the essays of Michel de Montaigne. Montaigne was a 16th century French nobleman who, at the age of 37, withdrew from public life to spend the rest of his life writing his autobiographical comics.

"FURTHERMORE, I HAVE ORDERED MYSELF TO DARE TO SAY ALL THAT I DARE TO DO, AND I DISLIKE EVEN THOUGHTS THAT ARE UNPUBLISHABLE."

(this was before comics had pictures).

(I have to read aloud to retain it).

Montaigne lived in a time of near constant civil war, and his writings often used battle scenes to illustrate personal situations in daily life.

"EMPEROR CONRAD III, HAVING BESIEGED GUELPH, WOULD NOT COME DOWN IN MILDER TERMS, THAN TO ALLOW THE GENTLEWOMEN BESIEGED WITH THE DUKE TO GO OUT, THEIR HONOR SAFE, ON FOOT, WITH WHAT THEY COULD CARRY AWAY ON THEM. THEY, GREAT-HEARTEDLY, LOADED THEIR HUSBANDS, THEIR CHILDREN AND THE DUKE HIMSELF ON THEIR SHOULDERS."

I don't know what's harder, reading Montaigne or reading **about** Montaigne. In the first page of this introduction alone there's the words epistemological, ontological, and exigencies. By the time I've looked up exigencies I've already forgotten what epistemological means, and I'm trying so hard to grasp it that I've long since lost the original point.

Also there's no dictionary here, just my "smart" phone, and it takes ten times longer to look up a word. Technology has brought me backwards.

But mostly I'm reading Philip Roth. I'm working my way through the Zuckerman novels, which are about a great and celebrated author and the tribulations of being a great and celebrated author. Basically it's a long-winded complainy humble-brag.

"NATHAN, YOU'RE NO LONGER THE EGGHEAD KID I PLUCKED FROM THE PAGES OF ESQUIRE. YOU HAVE ACHIEVED A SUCCESS AS ONLY A HANDFUL OF WRITERS EVER DO. SO STOP ACTING LIKE YOU DON'T."

And yet it's so good! I gobble it up in chunks. I consume it greedily. I can't get enough. And it makes me so jealous.

WHY DOES HE GET TO BE PHILIP ROTH AND NOT ME?!

IT'S BECAUSE HE'S A MAN, THAT'S WHY!

IF I WAS A MAN I'D TOTALLY BE PHILIP ROTH!

# Wednesday, July seventeenth

Every night I get scared.

Feels like something is crawling on me.

I feel so alone in this town.

I hear unfamiliar noises.

CREAK
THUMP

What am I doing here?

Ha, Ha, suckers! I've escaped!

# Thursday, July eighteenth

It is so hot. I am trying everything short of getting air conditioning to cool down.

I can't be the first person to have tried this.

This works better.

There is nothing to do here but read Montaigne.

Oh, who am I kidding. I can't read him. Instead I read this book How to Live, a self-help book about Montaigne. Or, Montaigne for babies.

I wish I could read Montaigne. I wish I could read the whole history of philosophy. I wish I could read French and Latin. I wish I could understand the way a person in the 16th century thought compared to how we think now.

SCIENCE?

GOD?

But more than that, I wish I could hold still. Stop twitching, stop interrupting myself. I wish I had exactly as much patience as it takes to exist. I wish I could experience experience.

THEY WANT TO GET OUT OF THEM-SELVES AND ESCAPE FROM THE MAN: THAT IS MADNESS. INSTEAD OF CHANGING INTO ANGELS THEY CHANGE INTO BEASTS.

## Friday, July nineteenth

Hey! I found a copy of the Tao Te Ching!

RESPONSIBILITY FOR ADULTS

REALITY FOR CARTOONISTS

FREE

To tell the truth, I would not be able to enjoy this solitary life without regular texting with Steve.

FILL YOUR BOWL TO THE BRIM AND IT WILL SPILL. KEEP SHARPENING THE KNIFE AND IT WILL BE BLUNT. CHASE AFTER MONEY AND SECURITY AND YOUR HEART WILL NEVER UNCLENCH.

Without him, I'd become too dark, too morbid, too lonely. He's been my link to humanity lately.

Tied to him, I'm free.

CARE ABOUT OTHER PEOPLE'S APPROVAL AND YOU WILL BE THEIR PRISONER. DO YOUR WORK, THEN STEP BACK. THE ONLY PATH TO SERENITY.

WHAT DOES IT SAY ABOUT STAYING IN YOUR APARTMENT FOR DAYS NOT SEEING ANYONE?

LET ME CHECK.

FLIP READ

OTHER PEOPLE ARE BRIGHT; I ALONE AM DARK. OTHER PEOPLE ARE SHARP; I ALONE AM DULL. OTHER PEOPLE HAVE A PURPOSE; I ALONE DON'T KNOW. I DRIFT LIKE A WAVE ON THE OCEAN, I BLOW AS AIMLESS AS THE WIND.

# Saturday, July Twentieth

I took a trip to Manhattan to spend a day, where Steve and I went to the Paul McCarthy show at the Armory.

SO YOU KNOW, THIS EXHIBITION CONTAINS EXPLICIT IMAGERY AND MATURE CONTENT.

GOT IT.

HOW DID YOU LEARN ABOUT THIS EVENT?

FROM HIM.

FROM A PORN SITE.

DID HE SAY PORN SITE?

THINK SO?

---

I don't feel like drawing it, so I will try to describe it: Big screens lining the walls depicting an orgiastic, violent, out-of-control party with Walt (Disney), "White Snow" and the seven depraved frat boys. A gross-looking fake forest and the house in which the debauchery took place, filled with the party's detritus and a fake dead Walt and White Snow.

HEY! MY FRIENDS ARE HERE!

---

In adjoining rooms, screens depicted disturbing powerplays between Walt and White. While Steve chatted with his friends, I chose a relatively benign one to sit and watch. But the endless groans, shrieks, grunts and wails coming from everywhere got to me.

GASP!

UNG UNG UNG UNG UNG HA HA OOOH GROAN PANT

---

We were there for hours, in spite of my revulsion and horror. Why? Because it was Art. Because air conditioning. Because we'd spent a lot on it. And because, beneath the repugnance, it was fascinating and special.

UNG GROAN OH!

DO YOU HAVE PTSD FROM WORKING HERE?

HAA HUH HUH UGH UN

SECURITY

---

Outside, the overpowering heat flattened us. Nothing to do but go to the park and speak about the end of humanity.

ON TV THE SCIENTISTS HAVE TO SAY WE'RE DOOMED UNLESS WE MAKE A CHANGE RIGHT AWAY. THE TRUTH IS WE'RE JUST DOOMED. THEY CAN'T SAY THAT.

---

COLLECTIVELY, WE ACT IRRATIONALLY, EVEN IF WE INDIVIDUALLY ACT RATIONALLY. I'LL SPEND HOURS SEPARATING MY RECYCLING AND COMPOSTING, BUT I MIGHT AS WELL USE THAT TIME TO PURSUE MY OWN INTERESTS. IN THE CONTEXT OF THE WORLD AS IT IS, I'M ACTING IRRATIONALLY.

IT'S TRUE. A PSYCHIATRIST MIGHT SAY THAT'S NEUROTIC BEHAVIOR.

Sunday, July twenty first

A freight train was derailed on the tracks, all the trains going North are suspended, and I'm derailed in the city.

That wouldn't have been a problem except my brother was arriving from South Korea with his girlfriend to stay for the weekend.

LET ME JUST GET MY STUFF OUT OF MY ROOM.

Nothing to do but go to a bar and reminisce.

I CAN'T BELIEVE YOU'RE THIRTY! YOU'RE SO OLD!

OH, THANKS!

IN MY MIND YOU'LL ALWAYS BE EIGHT OR NINE. WHICH IS I GUESS WHEN YOU GUYS LEFT. OR I LEFT. OR WHATEVER HAPPENED.

ANYWAY, THIRTY IS A GOOD AGE!

We watched a lightning storm from the pier.

WHERE IS STEVE? THIS IS AMAZING!

Steve was derailed by some sort of disaster at work.

I'M SORRY I MISSED THE LIGHTNING STORM.

IT'S OKAY, IT WAS DUMB.

I slept in my living room, roommates and guests passing all night.

# Monday, July Twenty-second

I am what you might call "self-educated." Which means I've been educated by an uneducated person (myself).

I'M STUCK HERE! THE TRAIN'S NOT RUNNING UNTIL TOMORROW. AND THE G TRAIN'S NOT RUNNING EITHER, SO I CAN'T GO TO STEVE'S.

I'LL GIVE YOU A RIDE HOME IN THE MORNING.

I am spending all of my time marking the passing time.

I'D WAIT BUT I NEED TO GO BACK FOR MY COMICS...

I DON'T READ YOUR COMICS.

YOU'VE TOLD ME THAT BEFORE.

BECAUSE IF YOU TALK ABOUT YOUR COMICS, I WON'T KNOW WHAT YOU'RE REFERRING TO.

Am I mentally ill? Or am I just coping with life's complexities like anyone else?

BUT IT SOUNDS LIKE YOU WANT TO TELL ME WHY YOU DON'T READ THEM.

THEY MAKE ME FEEL BAD.

BUT PEOPLE ARE ALWAYS TALKING TO ME ABOUT THEM. THEY'LL SAY, "DID IT REALLY HAPPEN THAT WAY?" I KNOW MORE ABOUT YOUR COMICS THROUGH OTHER PEOPLE.

The mental illness question had been a thing I'd been working out with my therapist. But that's over now.

THEY SAY IT'S ALL, "I'M CRAZY! I WANT TO BE ALONE! I'M CRAZY! LEAVE ME ALONE!"

AND THAT IF YOU REALLY WANT TO BE ALONE WHY DON'T YOU JUST GO BE ALONE.

WHO SAID THAT!?

NOBODY.

I'll have to rely on my own methods of coping now, like yoga, meditation, "journaling", talking to friends, reading...

WHO SAID IT?!

WAS IT ▓▓?! WAS IT ▓▓?

I DON'T REMEMBER.

Can a mentally ill person be healed by a person who is mentally ill (themself)?

YOU KNOW, PEOPLE SAY LOUSY THINGS ABOUT YOU AND I DON'T REPEAT THEM TO YOU!

I'M SORRY. I GUESS I WAS FEELING MEAN.

Tuesday, July twenty third

Early the next morning, Tony gave me a lift back.

LOOK AT THOSE TREES! SO LUSH! THEY LOOK LIKE THEY'RE GONNA SWALLOW US UP.

I KNOW. THEY'LL ALL BE GRAY STICKS IN SIX MONTHS.

I GUESS THAT GOES TO SHOW... SOMETHING OR OTHER.

PEOPLE ARE LIKE, 'I WANT IT TO BE THIS WEATHER ALL THE TIME' SO THEY MOVE TO LOS ANGELES AND THEN THEY'RE LIKE, "I WANT TO HAVE THIS FACE ALL THE TIME", THEN THEY GET PLASTIC SURGERY.

"WE DIDN'T NEED DIALOGUE, WE HAD FACES!"

He helped me to rearrange some things.

IT'S JUST, I CAME UP HERE PARTLY TO BE INDEPENDENT. I DEPEND TOO MUCH ON YOU.

I KNOW. YOU WANT TO GET AWAY FROM ME. YOU KEEP SAYING THAT.

SORRY.

THIS IS WOBBLY. I'LL FIX IT. CAN YOU GET ME THE SCREW-DRIVER?

I DIDN'T MEAN IT THAT WAY THOUGH. I MEANT I WAS GETTING AWAY FROM *US*.

THANKS. WE MIGHT JUST HAVE TO PROP THIS AGAINST THE BEAM.

DO YOU WANT A SANDWICH?

YES. I HAVEN'T HAD BREAKFAST.

Every time I am alone again I have to indulge in a lot of spacing out.

*friday, July twenty-sixth*

Oh no! It's seven PM and what have I been doing all day?! Not drawing comics, I'll tell you that.

The other day at the health food store I got some free samples of some sort of energy tablet which made me feel unexpectedly peppy.

HEY! I DON'T FEEL MY USUAL CRIPPLING SELF DOUBT TODAY!

I went back to the store but they didn't have the product.

THIS STUFF HAS SIMILAR INGREDIENTS. IT'S HIGHLY RECOMMENDED, EVEN FOR PEOPLE WITH ALZHEIMER'S.

"BRAIN BOOSTER..."

THIS ONE WOMAN TRIED IT AND SAID SHE STARTED REMEMBERING MEMORIES SHE DIDN'T KNOW SHE HAD.

I didn't buy it, it sounded too much like a snake oil remedy spiel, and it was expensive.

OH, COME ON! WHAT A PITCH.

STILL...THAT'D BE PRETTY COOL TO RECOVER FORGOTTEN MEMORIES...

I went back again. The key ingredient of both products was rhodiola rosea. I bought a bottle of capsules of that, more concentrated and less expensive.

I guess the high concentration created the opposite effect of what I was going for.

I SHOULD GET UP AND TURN ON THE LIGHTS...

...HOW LONG HAVE I BEEN SITTING HERE? TEN MINUTES? SIX HOURS?

WAIT, WHAT WAS I THINKING JUST NOW?

I SHOULD GET UP.

# Saturday, July Twenty-seventh

So I broke down and bought a bottle of that "Brain Booster."

NATURAL
OODS

And suddenly remembered where I'd left my car.

Fortunately I also remembered my AAA number.

I was worried that Gordon was going to be pissed.

GABRIELLE! YOU CAME BACK TO ME! I'M SO RELIEVED!

I PROMISE I'LL DO RIGHT BY YOU FROM NOW ON!

But I was back in the bosom of my family.

MOMMY!

HEY, MA.

Until the Brain Booster wore off.

UMM... IS THIS SOMEONE'S BABY?

I THINK IT POOPED...

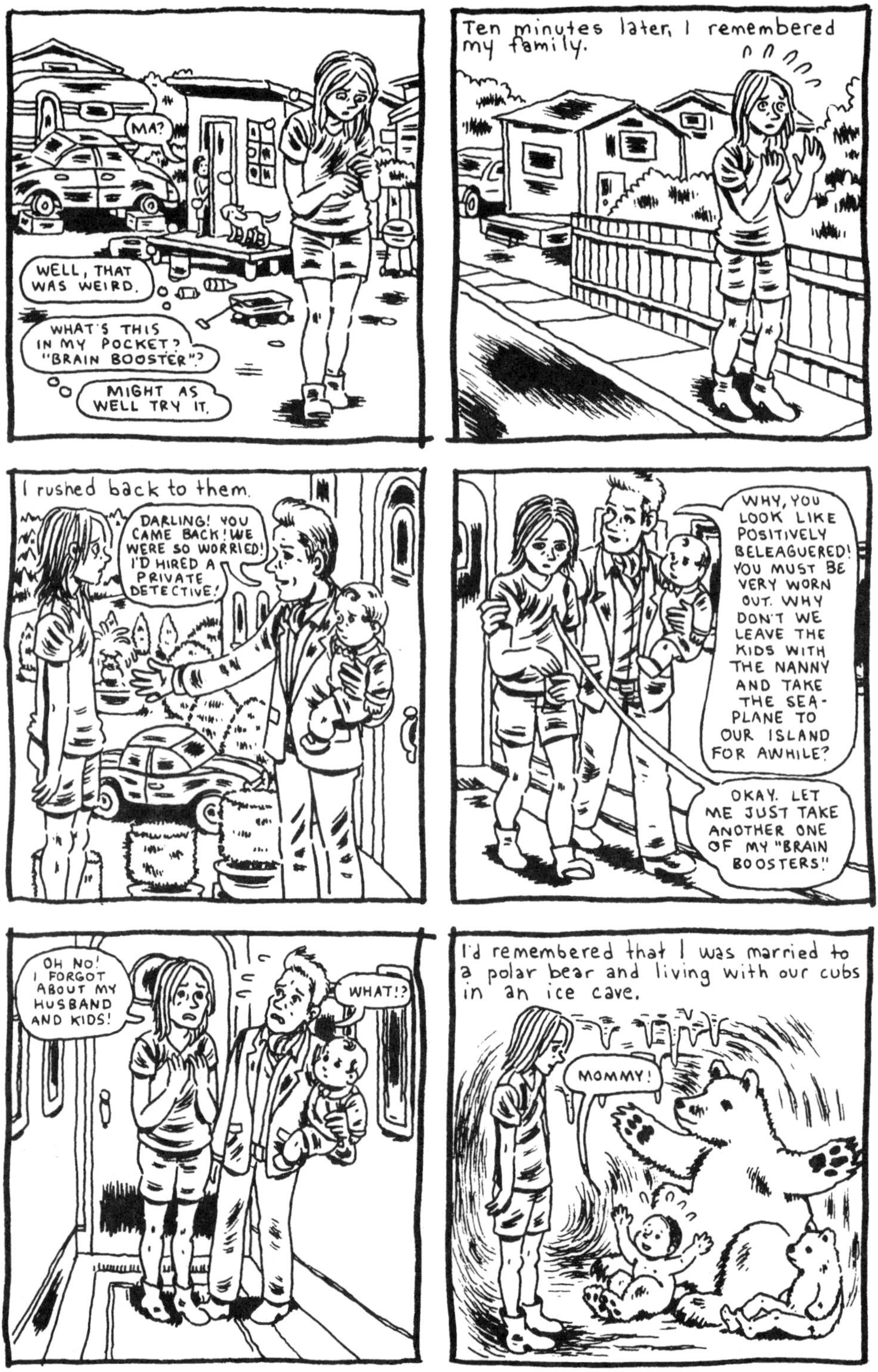
MA?
WELL, THAT WAS WEIRD.
WHAT'S THIS IN MY POCKET? "BRAIN BOOSTER"?
MIGHT AS WELL TRY IT.
Ten minutes later, I remembered my family.
I rushed back to them.
DARLING! YOU CAME BACK! WE WERE SO WORRIED! I'D HIRED A PRIVATE DETECTIVE!
WHY, YOU LOOK LIKE POSITIVELY BELEAGUERED! YOU MUST BE VERY WORN OUT. WHY DON'T WE LEAVE THE KIDS WITH THE NANNY AND TAKE THE SEA-PLANE TO OUR ISLAND FOR AWHILE?
OKAY. LET ME JUST TAKE ANOTHER ONE OF MY "BRAIN BOOSTERS."
OH NO! I FORGOT ABOUT MY HUSBAND AND KIDS!
WHAT!?
I'd remembered that I was married to a polar bear and living with our cubs in an ice cave.
MOMMY!

I had to get out of there. This Brain Booster was nothing but trouble.

I needed to lay low for awhile. I rented a little apartment in a Victorian house that went for cheap because the previous tenant had mysteriously disappeared.

OH, NO! I FORGOT TO DRAW MY DIARY COMICS!

AND NOTHING HAS HAPPENED AT ALL!

WAIT A MINUTE! I DON'T HAVE TO DO THIS! NO ONE'S MAKING ME!

ARE YOU STILL HERE?

GO AWAY! I WANNA BE ALONE!

DON'T YOU HAVE ANY RESPECT FOR PRIVACY?

GET OUT!

SLAM!

NO, WAIT, DON'T GO!

IT GETS SCARY HERE AT NIGHT!

ARE YOU MAD AT ME?

Tuesday, July thirtieth

I hate to admit it but this new smartphone of mine is becoming a problem. I suppose it's because I am lonely here, and, despite all that I get, starving for love.

TWENTY-TWO LIKES! DOES THAT EQUAL LOVE?

Then there's the general malaise, which is exactly what I'd meant to escape from in the city. I could think of nothing to do about it but go for a walk without my phone.

LOOK AT THESE HOUSES.

Life is vivid when there is no means of recording it.

I found an estate sale. I was hoping to find a round table for the porch.

I found one that was only five dollars.

DO YOU THINK I COULD BORROW THAT HANDTRUCK?

A man and his daughter offered me and my table a ride, and the seller's son loaded it in the car.

IT WON'T GO ALL THE WAY IN.

SURE IT WILL. TURN IT SIDE-WAYS. TO YOUR LEFT.

OH.

We had to disassemble the legs to get it into the car.

OOPS!

WAS THAT A WASHER OR A BOLT?

WASHER.

WE'LL GET YOU ANOTHER ONE. WASHERS ARE NO PROBLEM. BOLTS ARE HARDER TO REPLACE.

YOU'RE VERY PROFESSIONAL. WHERE DOES THIS STUFF COME FROM?

SHUT!

WHEN PEOPLE MOVE FAR AWAY AND DON'T WANT TO DEAL WITH ALL THEIR OLD STUFF, WE TAKE CARE OF IT FOR THEM.

The guy who gave me a ride helped me carry it to the porch.

I assembled and scrubbed it clean. It must have been sitting in a garage for a long time.

It was in perfect shape, except for one single cigarette burn. Perhaps from a sleepless night, a housewife sitting up for someone who didn't come home, many years before she'd "move far away."

It is a good, sturdy table from an era long before smartphones.

Festival Entreviñetas, Bogotá & Medellín, Colombia,
September 14th-22nd 2013

Saturday, September 14th, 2013

Welcome to Gabrielle Bell's Diary of Colombia. Miss Bell has employed me to depict her experiences. I will do my best to approximate her stlye. She is seated a couple seats ahead, waiting for the Xanax to kick in.

Miss Bell got the idea of hiring a secretary to keep her diary when she read that Michel de Montaigne, during some of his travels, did so, in order to participate more fully in the life around him.

CAN I HAVE HER DESSERT?

Miss Bell believes that because he retired from public life to write his semi-auto-biographical Essays at the age of 37, the age which she is now, she and Montaigne have much in common.

LISTEN TO THIS: "I MAKE SILLY AND STUPID REMARKS UNWORTHY OF A CHILD, I HAVE A DREAMY WAY OF WITHDRAWING INTO MYSELF AND A DULL AND CHILDISH IGNORANCE OF COMMON THINGS."

That she has yet to read The Essays does not deter her.

IF I READ TWO PAGES A DAY I'LL HAVE READ ALL FOURTEEN HUNDRED PAGES IN ABOUT TWO YEARS... OR I COULD DO FOUR PAGES IN ONE YEAR, OR ONE PAGE IN FOUR...

She overlooks the fact that Montaigne was a nobleman, a magistrate and a soldier, spoke several languages and actually read the great works, and not just the dirty parts.

HEE HEE! "WHEN THE CAPRICIOUS VEIN THROBS IN THE RESTLESS MEMBER, EJECT THE GATHERED SPERM IN ANYTHING AT ALL."

In preparation for this employment, I have read the complete Essays, and I must say this: those travelogues by that anonymous servant comprised the most compelling, well-written prose of the entire book. That he or she went nameless and uncredited is a travesty.

Miss Bell was greeted at the airport by some friendly people holding a sign with her name on it, which was the sweetest gratification she could imagine. Mr. Kuper, also an American artist traveling with Miss Bell, was equally honored.

MUCHO GUSTO!

Miss Bell piled into a tiny car with Miss Acosta and Mr. Rodriguez, who were the festival's interpreters, and did her best to endear herself to them.

IT'S SO LUSH AND GREEN!

HA, HA! THAT'S WHAT EVERYONE SAYS WHEN THEY FIRST ARRIVE HERE.

OH, LET ME TRY AGAIN... WHAT KIND OF ANIMALS CAN ONE SEE AROUND HERE? IGUANAS?

Mr. Rodriguez told the visitors a little bit about the city.

MEDELLÍN HAS A SOCIAL STRATIFICATION SYSTEM THAT DIVIDES THE CITY INTO SIX DISTRICTS ON A SCALE OF POVERTY TO WEALTH, WITH THE FIRST BEING THE POOREST. YOU'RE STAYING IN EL POBLADO, WHICH IS THE SIXTH.

At the hotel, Miss Bell realized just how helpless she was, not knowing the language.

QUICK, CAN YOU TEACH ME SPANISH RIGHT NOW?

TO START, WHAT WAS THAT PHRASE YOU SAY WHEN YOU MEET? MUCHOS BUENOS?

¡MUCHO GUSTO!

ALSO, HOW DO I SAY I'M SORRY?

In her room, in an attempt to locate an aspirin, Miss Bell emptied the contents of her luggage onto her bed and fell asleep in the nest she'd created.

As for me, I caught a bus that took a ten-hour detour to Bogotá and back, and joined the party later in the night.

Later, Miss Bell rejoined Mr. Rodriguez and Miss Acosta at an event for Inu Waters.

WHENEVER I TRY TO SPEAK A SPANISH WORD, A FRENCH WORD COMES UP, WHICH IS THE OPPOSITE OF WHAT HAPPENS WHEN I'M IN FRANCE.

A LOT OF THE TIME I HAVE TROUBLE SPEAKING ENGLISH.

I CAN SEE THAT. YOU SEEM VERY SHY.

When her shyness is pointed out to her, Miss Bell grows even more so; her cover is blown.

I'D THOUGHT I'D MANAGED TO HIDE THAT...

WE SHOULD GO SEE INU.

Miss Bell was glad to find that wherever she goes, there are always scruffy, bespectacled cartoonists to exchange sketchbooks and draw with.

WHAT ARE THEY SAYING?

THAT INU WAS THE FIRST ARTIST IN COLOMBIA TO MAKE MINI-COMICS... NOT EXACTLY THE FIRST, BUT-SHOULD I TRANSLATE EVERYTHING?

HOW ABOUT JUST THE MOST INTERESTING STUFF?

OKAY...HE'S WORKING ON A PORNO-GRAPHIC ANTHOLOGY...

Walking back to the hotel with a festival organizer, Miss Bell felt frightened.

I DON'T KNOW THIS AREA SO WELL...MAYBE WE SHOULD TAKE A CAB.

When Miss Bell returned, she found Miss Acosta waiting in the hotel lobby. Her suitcase had been locked in an office till morning and she hadn't yet learned where she would stay.

ONE OF THE ORGANIZERS QUIT AT THE LAST MINUTE AND THEY'RE VERY UNDERSTAFFED.

Later still, Miss Acosta learned she'd be staying at a youth hostel elsewhere.

NO TENGO PIJAMA.

Sunday, September 15th

The first thing Miss Bell did was find a comfortable cafe to sit alone at. Next, she asked herself: What would Montaigne do?

He would meet with the most important personages and intellectuals of the city, remark on the idiosyncrasies of the local customs, and try to find a regional cure for his kidney stones, she concluded.

Miss Bell spent the rest of the afternoon googling Pablo Escobar.

Later, she joined Miss Acosta in a cab to the Parque Explora. The night before, someone had moved Miss Acosta's suitcase out of the office it'd been stored in and it was stolen.

I HAD ALL MY BEST THINGS IN IT.

... A RING THAT MY FAVORITE PROFESSOR BROUGHT ME FROM THAILAND FOR MY GRADUATION PRESENT.

IT'S TERRIBLE! WHAT ARE YOU GOING TO DO?

I GUESS I'LL HAVE TO QUIT. I'VE BEEN WEARING THE SAME CLOTHES SINCE I LEFT BOGOTÁ AND I'VE GOT NOTHING TO CHANGE INTO.

WHAT DOES THAT SIGN SAY?

"DON'T LITTER."

THEY THINK PUTTING UP A BILLBOARD IS GONNA CHANGE THE WAY PEOPLE THINK.

PEOPLE HAVE NO SENSE OF SOCIAL RESPONSIBILITY HERE. EVERYONE ASSUMES SOMEONE ELSE WILL FIX THINGS.

COLOMBIANS HAVE A SAYING- "ESO NO PASA NADA." - "NOTHING'S GONNA HAPPEN." IT'S A WAY OF TEMPTING FATE.

IS THAT A CYNICAL ATTITUDE? OR AN OPTIMISTIC ONE?

I DON'T KNOW.

IS IT BECAUSE OF PABLO ESCOBAR?

I WAS A KID WHEN ALL THAT WAS HAPPENING. I DON'T KNOW WHAT COLOMBIA WAS LIKE BEFORE ESCOBAR.

HE HAD A COMPLICATED IMPACT ON COLOMBIA. AT THE SAME TIME AS HE WAS TERRORIZING THE COUNTRY, HE STYLED HIMSELF AS THIS ROBIN HOOD FIGURE.

HE BUILT HOUSING AND SOCCER FIELDS FOR THE POOR ...

HE'D DRIVE AROUND IN BUSES AND GIVE OUT WASHING MACHINES OR TVS OR CASH.

SO THE POOR KIDS WANT TO GROW UP TO BE MERCENARIES AND DRUG LORDS. THE GIRLS WANT TO GROW UP TO BE THEIR MISTRESSES.

I READ THAT ESCOBAR'S OLD ESTATE IS A THEME PARK NOW.

YEAH, A WATER PARK. MY COUSIN WENT. IT'S WEIRD.

CAN WE GO THERE?

I GUESS IT'S POSSIBLE. IT'S ABOUT TWO HOURS AWAY. THERE'S PROBABLY A BUS THAT GOES THERE. BUT I'VE GOT WORK...

YOU SAID YOU WERE QUITTING! HOW ARE YOU GONNA WORK WITHOUT YOUR THINGS?

OH YEAH! I'M QUITTING!

HOW ABOUT TOMORROW?

SURE! BUT I DON'T HAVE A BATHING SUIT...

I WILL BUY YOU ONE! FOR TAKING ME.

OKAY THEN! WHY NOT?!

They went to the planetarium of the Parque Explora, an interactive science museum that aims to promote social change. Admission is on a sliding scale: those from the 6th district pay the most, while people from the first pay nothing.

ARE WE GOING TO SEE THE FISHES?

YOU'RE THINKING AQUARIUM. THIS IS STARS.

It also hosted the visiting cartoonists. Miss Bell attended a panel discussion for Mr. Kuper, expecting it to be in English.

SI VIVÍ EN OAXACA POR DOS AÑOS, SE FUE UN TIEMPO MUY INTERESANTE

Miss Acosta slipped in to tell Miss Bell some good news.

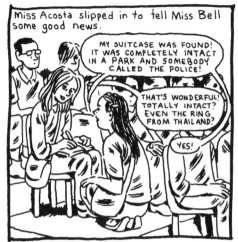

MY SUITCASE WAS FOUND! IT WAS COMPLETELY INTACT IN A PARK AND SOMEBODY CALLED THE POLICE!

THAT'S WONDERFUL! TOTALLY INTACT? EVEN THE RING FROM THAILAND?

YES!

SO I GUESS I CAN'T GO TO THE WATERPARK, BECAUSE I'M NOT QUITTING AFTER ALL.

I'M JUST SO GLAD FOR YOU. IT MUST BE SUCH A RELIEF.

IT'S FUNNY, THE PARK THEY FOUND IT IN TRANSLATES AS "WISH PARK"!

Miss Bell was very happy for Miss Acosta.

When she stepped out of the auditorium, Miss Bell realized at what loose ends she was. Her colleagues were preoccupied with presentations she couldn't understand, and Miss Acosta was speaking with an older gentleman at the café. Making a valiant effort to appear nonchalant, she exited the building.

Outside, an enormous crowd had gathered to watch a projection of a Miyazaki film. As far as Miss Bell's vision could reach, children played, couples necked, and grandparents reclined.

Medellín is in the shape of a gigantic bowl, with millions of houses packed onto the mountainsides in every direction. At night when the lights are on it is dazzling to distraction.

GABRIELLE!

THERE YOU ARE!

THIS IS MY UNCLE MANUEL. HE CAME TO CONSOLE ME FOR MY LOST SUITCASE BUT INSTEAD WE'RE CELEBRATING

I JUST REALIZED YOU DON'T HAVE A RIDE BACK.

Miss Bell was beginning to realize she was not Montaigne.

I'M GLAD WE FOUND YOU! I DON'T KNOW HOW YOU WOULD'VE GOTTEN BACK.

I COULD ALWAYS HAVE TAKEN A CAB.

OH, YOU CAN'T JUST HAIL A CAB AROUND HERE. IT COULD BE DANGEROUS. YOU HAVE TO GO TO A DESIGNATED PLACE AND GET A NUMBER.

Miss Acosta and Mr. Sanabria invited Miss Bell to dine. Miss Bell grew embarrassed when she ordered a more expensive meal and Mr. Sanabria insisted on paying.

NO, PLEASE...

COLOMBIAN HOSPITALITY!

Poor Miss Bell, trying too hard to entertain, to show her gratitude. It makes for an awkwardness that undermines her whole intention.

MY FIRST COLOMBIAN MEAL!

WOULD YOU LIKE ME TO TAKE A PICTURE?

AND I'LL TAKE ONE OF YOUR MILLIONTH COLOMBIAN MEALS.

Miss Bell was grateful, however, not just for the meal and the ride, but for the company.

IT'S SUCH A MYSTERY ABOUT YOUR SUITCASE. WHY WOULD SOMEBODY STEAL IT JUST TO LEAVE IT UNTOUCHED IN THE PARK?

AND THEN SOMEONE ELSE FOUND IT AND CALLED THE POLICE!

As for me, I hailed a cab, got robbed, beaten, left for dead on the side of the highway, and walked the rest of the way back to the hotel.

Monday, September 16th

Miss Bell accompanied several cartoonists on the metrocable, watching the run-down comunas crammed into the mountainside below.

From the station they walked to the sleek modernist Biblioteca España, surrounded by the ramshackle first district streets.

They spoke about their work to a handful of local residents. At the end a teacher asked what she could do about a student who, instead of studying, would fill his worksheets with drawings.

Miss Bell's initial impulse was to say to let the kid draw, but then she reflected on her own schooling. She was very bad at math, and drawing was a soothing anti-dote to her frustration.

HOW DOES "Y" EQUAL THREE? IT MAKES NO SENSE! IT'S A LETTER!

I CAN'T ASK AGAIN. HE'S ALREADY EXPLAINED IT TO ME TWICE!

THIS IS SUCH A BEAUTIFUL CURVING LINE. I WILL TURN IT INTO A MUSHROOM.

Until fifth grade, Miss Bell enjoyed math. Although she was slower than the others, she derived satisfaction from solving these tangible, black and white problems.

In fifth grade, she got stuck on fractions. She was placed in special ed and enjoyed the undivided attention of her tutor, who talked her through each daunting step of dividing up the number one.

NOW WHAT DO YOU DO WITH THE REMAINING FOUR?

OH, RIGHT! I CARRY IT OVER.

Miss Bell realized something. Up until fifth grade, all her math teachers had been women. After that, it was always men, and that is when she began to fail.

Miss Bell was afraid of men. She would ask a question about the assignment, then not listen to the answer. Instead, she would stare at Mr. Hoxie's mustache or Mr. Berry's adam's apple and wonder what he thought of her.

He would get exasperated, and she would grow more afraid, and eventually they would both give up. She hoped to at least impress him with her elaborate, psychedelic drawings.

Twenty years later, Miss Bell is a moderately successful cartoonist, but she struggles each month to make ends meet. She suspects this has to do with her vague, intuitive approach to dividing, subtracting and multiplying numbers.

Miss Bell concluded that the way to bring a child's natural curiosity to their work was to lend copious amounts of patience and attention to the areas of their difficulty. Furthermore, the student would need to be assured that they wouldn't be scolded or ridiculed if they didn't understand right away.

But by the time she gathered her thoughts, she was already on her way back down the mountain.

## Tuesday, September 17th

Miss Bell attempted to phone Mr. Rodriguez to acquire directions to the evening's event, but was unable to summon a proper dial tone.

BEEP BEEP
BEEP BEEP
BEEP

She had no choice but to go it alone. The problem was that she had an address but no name. Another problem was that she'd scrawled two other addresses on the same paper. Miss Bell's solution was to visit all three locations, processing by elimination.

After exhausting her possibilities, Miss Bell returned to the hotel and attempted to enlist the receptionist in helping her to phone Mr. Rodriguez.

JE SUIS...

ER, YO ESTOY...

Miss Bell did not ask correctly, or perhaps not nicely enough, and was rebuffed. Attempting a retreat to her room upstairs, she was blocked by men laying carpet.

Crossing the lobby to the elevator, Miss Bell discovered she'd collected an audience.

EXCUSE ME, THE ELEVATOR IS BROKEN.

Why Miss Bell chose to make things more difficult for everyone by not acquiring a three dollar sim card for her cell phone is a mystery to me, but I trust she has her reasons.

EXCUSE ME.

When she finally found the venue (Its name, Calle 9+1, she'd mistaken for the address), Miss Bell was met with no fanfare.

OH, HI GABRIELLE! YOU SAID TO TRANSLATE WHEN ANYTHING INTERESTING WAS SAID...

THERE'S A HEATED DISCUSSION GOING ON...

SHE IS SAYING, "COMICS ARE NOT A DOORWAY TO LITERATURE, THEY ARE LITERATURE."

HE SAYS: "THERE'S NO SHAME IN BEING A DOORWAY, IT'S STILL PART OF THE HOUSE," AND THAT HE LEARNED TO LOVE READING THROUGH COMIC BOOKS.

SHE SAYS THAT THEY'RE MORE THAN JUST A TOOL FOR LEARNING TO READ.

HE SAYS, "IF YOU CAN REACH SOMEONE LIKE ME WITH JUST GRAPHICS AND WORDS, THAT'S SOMETHING TO BE PROUD OF."

MANSPLAINING AT ITS FINEST!

Miss Bell joined Mr. Díaz, Miss Parra & Mr. Torres.

I WENT TO THIS CLUB RUN BY DRUG LORDS. THERE WERE BAGS OF COKE ON THE TABLE AND INFANTRY POLICEMEN STANDING AROUND WITH MACHINE GUNS.

THE OWNER WAS LIKE, 'YOU ARTISTS, YOU THINK YOU'RE SO SPECIAL, BUT I'M THE ONE WHO PULLS THE STRINGS AROUND HERE."

WERE YOU SCARED?

YES, I WAS SHAKING!

OH YOU'RE TALKING ABOUT TRANSFUSION. HE ALWAYS SAYS THAT! IT'S NOT SO BAD. I GO THERE ALL THE TIME.

DO YOU FEEL SAFE GOING THERE?

YEAH, THE NARCOS KEEP IT SAFE INSIDE. OUTSIDE YOU'VE GOT TO BE CAREFUL THOUGH.

AND THE MEN DON'T BOTHER YOU?

NAH, THEY'RE VERY RESPECTFUL.

DO YOU GO DANCING?

NO, IT'S NOT THAT KIND OF CLUB.

WHAT DO PEOPLE DO THERE?

OH, YOU KNOW, HANG OUT, TALK, LISTEN TO MUSIC.

AND YOU CAN BUY COKE THERE, TOO?

YES, OF COURSE.

HOW ABOUT COCA LEAVES? DO YOU KNOW WHERE TO GET THAT?

SURE, YOU CAN GET IT ANYWHERE.

There is a theory that Miss Bell's synapses don't transmit enough dopamine, and she is searching the world for a natural cure for her attention deficiency and chronic anxiety.

THE LADYS ON THE CORNER SELLING CANDY ALWAYS HAVE IT.

I DIDN'T THINK IT'D BE SO EASY.

Miss Bell has been working her way through the historical novels of Isabel Allende, from which she's learned about the Spanish Conquistadors' frustrated attempts to subdue the fierce, formidable, coca-chewing Mapuche Natives of Chile. It is Miss Bell's persistent folly to believe that the contents of books are equivalent to reality.

And so...

SORRY. SORRY.

HA HA! I THOUGHT YOU SAID COCALIC, WHICH I FIGURED WAS SOME AMERICAN SLANG FOR COCAINE.

IT WAS MY MISTAKE! I BROUGHT UP COCA LEAVES OUT OF NOWHERE.

COCA LEAVES AREN'T SO EASY TO GET AROUND HERE.

They returned to Calle 9+1.

DO YOU LIKE TO DANCE?

SOMETIMES. WHAT KIND OF MUSIC DO YOU LIKE?

I DON'T KNOW. BRIAN ENO?

YOU SHOULD TRY GUANABANO. YOU'D LIKE THAT PLACE.

Miss Bell wished somebody would take her by the hand and insist that she dance.

COME AND DANCE! DON'T BE SHY!

CAN YOU TEACH ME HOW?

Miss Bell chided herself for not being more adventurous.

IT'S ALL IN THE HIPS. KEEP IT LOW.

LIKE THIS?

WHY DIDN'T I JUST GO ALONG WITH IT AND TRY THE COCALIC? WHAT'S THE WORST THAT COULD'VE HAPPENED?

## Wednesday, September 18th

Miss Bell met Miss Powerpoala in downtown Medellín.

MY RELATIVES SAY, "YOU WALK AROUND DOWNTOWN BY YOURSELF?"

BUT THEY LIVED HERE WHEN YOU'D HAVE TO KEEP YOUR WINDOWS TAPED IN CASE OF BOMBINGS.

I WALK THROUGH THE PARQUE DEL PERIODISTA AT THREE IN THE MORNING AND NO ONE BOTHERS ME.

IT'S NOT THAT IT ISN'T DANGEROUS. IT'S JUST THAT WE LIVE SIDE BY SIDE WITH VIOLENCE.

They cut through the Parque del Periodista, the cops-free zone, where you can see people spooning coke into their noses right out in the open.

THE DRUG DEALERS PAY THE COPS OFF AND POLICE THE AREA THEMSELVES.

At Guanabano, the bar recommended by Miss Parra the previous evening, Miss Bell and Miss Powerpoala drew the men at the next table, and then they drew each other, their arms wrapped around the men.

GIGGLE    HEE HEE

Several cartoonists joined them. As drawing roulettes took place and sketchbooks were exchanged, Miss Bell inquired of Mr. Noreña about the local policies.

SO AS LONG AS THEY BUY THE DRUGS FROM THE DEALERS WHO RUN THE PARK, IT'S ALL OKAY?

YES, THEY KEEP ORDER BUT YOU'VE GOTTA FOLLOW THEIR RULES.

HOW DO THEY KEEP ORDER?

IF THEY SEE SOMEONE MAKING TROUBLE, THEY GIVE THEM A WARNING. IT COULD JUST BE A LOOK.

AND IF THEY KEEP MAKING TROUBLE?

THEY'LL TAKE HIM AROUND THE CORNER AND BEAT HIM WITH BATS.

SO THE DRUG DEALERS ARE DOING TWO JOBS, DRUG DEALING AND LAW ENFORCEMENT?

YES.    AND THE POLICE DO NO JOB?

YES.    SO THE COPS USE THEIR EXTRA LEISURE TIME TO CONTEMPLATE LIFE AND REFLECT ON HOW TO BETTER SOCIETY?

I DON'T THINK YOU'VE GOT A CLEAR GRASP ON THE DEPTH OF THE CORRUPTION HERE.

## Thursday, September 19th

Miss Bell insists I draw a comic on this local flight, in spite of the extreme turbulence and my own fatigue. I was not issued a room during this trip, I simply waited in the lobby until Miss Bell had need of me.

The lurching back and forth of this craft from Medellín towards Bogotá is causing Miss Bell to contemplate the end of herself.

Miss Bell's travel companion, Mr. Restrepo, did not see the erratic flight as cause for alarm.

I WAS THINKING THAT IF THE PLANE CRASHED I WOULDN'T HAVE TO FINISH MY GRAPHIC NOVEL.

WHY ARE YOU SO TRAGIC?

In an attempt to calm Miss Bell, Mr. Restrepo shared many intimate, personal details from his life with her.

WHEN I WAS A KID I'D PUT A PENCIL IN MY NOSE TO MAKE MYSELF SNEEZE.

At the baggage claim, Miss Bell wondered if somebody would pick them up.

WHAT IF NO ONE COMES TO MEET US?

DON'T WORRY, I KNOW MY WAY AROUND! ALSO I AM FLUENT IN THE LANGUAGE.

But the two were met by a Mr. Morven.

I HEARD YOU WERE LOOKING FOR COCA LEAVES. I CAN TAKE YOU TO WHERE YOU CAN BUY SOME.

YES!

After dropping her luggage at the hotel, Mr. Morven accompanied Miss Bell to the store that sold coca leaves.

YOU HAVE TO CHEW IT CAREFULLY AND THINK ABOUT THE SPIRIT OF THE PLANT.

Miss Bell purchased a bag of coca leaves and a package of green-tinted coca leaf cookies.

¡MUCHAS GRACIAS!

CON MUCHO GUSTO.

Mr. Morven brought Miss Bell to the museum where the panels and workshops would take place, and ran into Miss Braud. The two women admired the work of Henning Wagenbreth.

THERE'S SO MUCH GOING ON IN HERE. LOOK AT ALL THE DESPAIR IN JUST THIS ONE LITTLE SQUARE!

WHY HAVE I NOT HEARD OF HIM?

HE'S FROM AN OLDER GENERATION THAN US.

THAT'S NICE TO KNOW.

I KNOW.

BUT IT FEELS VERY CONTEMPORARY.

Miss Bell and miss Braud went to a cafe, and Miss Bell proffered the coca leaf cookies. Miss Braud nibbled hers and found it disagreeable. Miss Bell gobbled up both cookies.

Mr. Morven accompanied Miss Bell back to her hotel so she could rest before her panel discussion later.

YOU WANT TO MAKE A LITTLE BALL IN THE SIDE OF YOUR MOUTH OUTSIDE OF YOUR TEETH.

Miss Bell was not sure if the cookie had any effect on her. She did notice that she felt giddy and happy and fullfilled, but she was pretty sure she felt that way all the time.

Miss Bell lost track of the time and suddenly it was time to go to her panel discussion with Miss Paola and Miss Tateé.

WHAT! NOW?

I JUST REALIZED I'D FINALLY SET MY CLOCK BACK AN HOUR TO COLOMBIA TIME TODAY BUT WAS STILL MENTALLY ADDING AN HOUR.

DOES THAT MAKE SENSE?

Miss Bell hurried to the event on an empty stomach, a sleepless night, and possibly intoxicated.

I HAVE A BITE SIZED CHOCOLATE BAR.

THAT WILL HAVE TO DO.

She found herself expected to say something about the internet and creativity.

I MEAN...THE INTERNET IS GOOD FOR SOME STUFF...BUT THEN SOMETIMES IT'S NOT...

Fortunately, Miss Acosta had a way of translating what Miss Bell MEANT to say.

"ESCRIBIR UN BLOG E INTERACTUAR EN REDES SOCIALES PUEDE SER BENEFICIOSO PARA UN ARTISTA QUE ESTÁ CONSTRUYENDO UNA AUDIENCIA Y FORMANDO UNA COMUNIDAD, PERO HACER SOLAMENTE ESTAS COSAS RARA VEZ TRAE COMPENSACIÓN ECONÓMICA Y, EN MI OPINIÓN, NO SUSTITUYE LA INTERACCIÓN SOCIAL A LA ANTIGUA O EL LIBRO IMPRESO."

*"BLOGGING AND SOCIAL NETWORKING CAN BE BENEFICIAL FOR AN ARTIST IN BUILDING AN AUDIENCE AND FORMING A COMMUNITY, BUT SIMPLY DOING THESE THINGS RARELY LEADS TO FINANCIAL COMPENSATION, AND, IN MY OPINION, IS NO SUBSTITUTE FOR OLD-FASHIONED SOCIAL INTERACTION OR THE PRINTED BOOK."

Miss Bell was caught off guard by a question spoken in perfect English.

THIS QUESTION IS FOR GABRIELLE: YOU SEEM TO BE EXTREMELY SHY.

HOW DO YOU MANAGE TO PROMOTE YOUR WORK IN SPITE OF YOUR OBVIOUS SOCIAL AWKWARDNESS?

Miss Bell attempted to make a joke, but at the same time tried to make a different joke. She felt her face doing things she didn't want it to do, as if she were having a stroke. She felt naked and ugly beneath the fluorescent lights, and yet she felt helplessly giddy.

I THOUGHT NO ONE NOTICED...

I'M GONNA GO NOW...

HA HA...

## Friday, September 20th

Miss Bell learned from the internet that she would need bicarbonate sodium to alkalize the coca. She used her toothpaste and made a ball of the mixture on the side of her mouth.

She thought it would be a good idea to eat something. Crossing the room to reach the bread and cheese she kept, she remembered that she hadn't yet finished getting dressed.

Reaching for her pants, she thought she ought to put the coca leaves away before they spilled.

Then she remembered that she was hungry. Eventually Miss Bell was simply walking around in circles.

Miss Bell had to take a long, hot shower to wash off the heebie-jeebies.

It was interrupted by a phone call. She'd forgotten she was to meet Miss Córdoba and Mr. Díaz in the lobby at eleven.

OH NO! I AM SORRY! I'LL BE RIGHT DOWN!

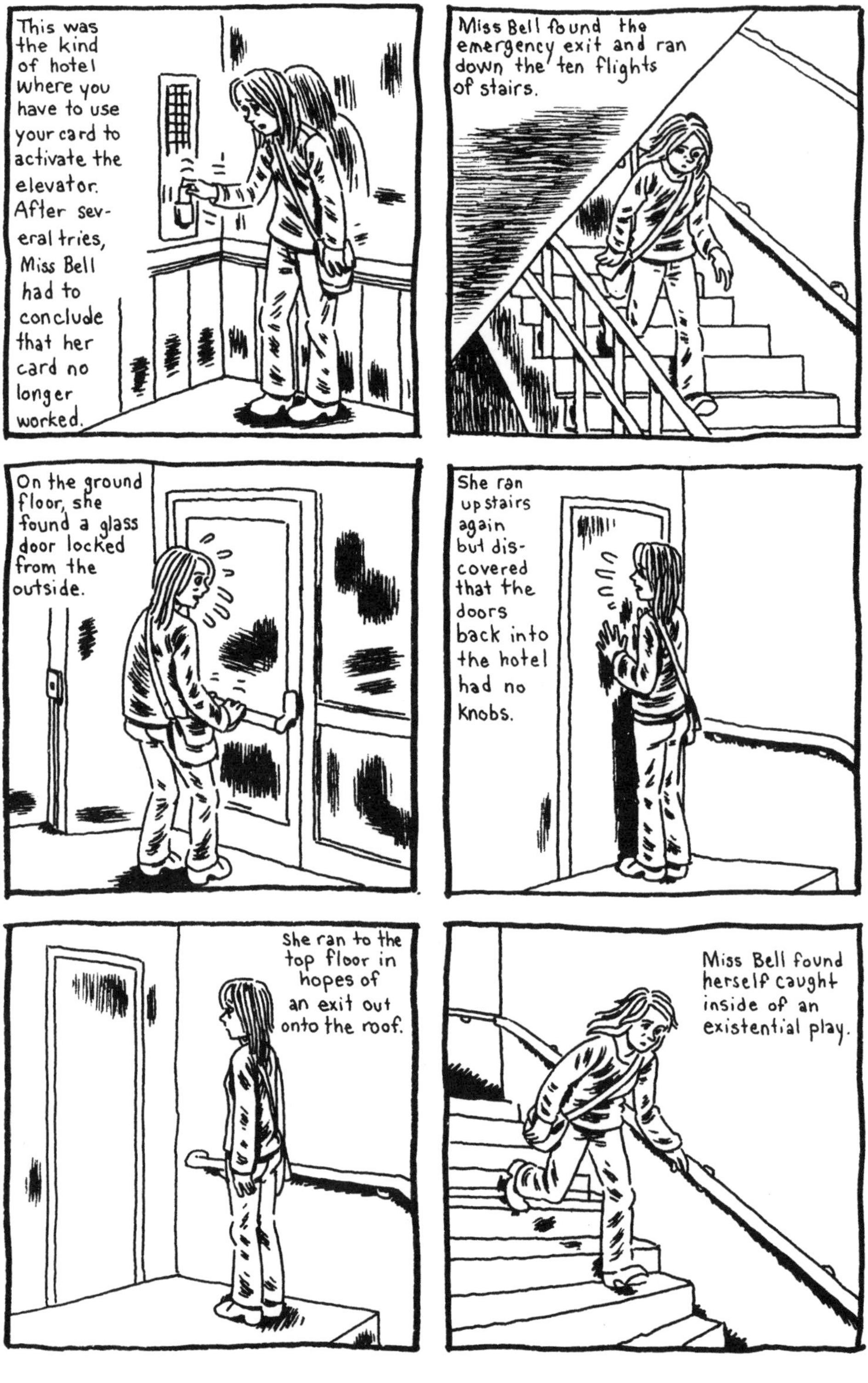
This was the kind of hotel where you have to use your card to activate the elevator. After several tries, Miss Bell had to conclude that her card no longer worked.
Miss Bell found the emergency exit and ran down the ten flights of stairs.
On the ground floor, she found a glass door locked from the outside.
She ran upstairs again but discovered that the doors back into the hotel had no knobs.
She ran to the top floor in hopes of an exit out onto the roof.
Miss Bell found herself caught inside of an existential play.

Back on the ground floor, Miss Bell noticed a button she hadn't seen before.

As she pressed the button, she wondered,

Press to here in case of emergency

Pulse en caso de emergencia

Was this really an emergency? Was her life in immediate jeopardy?

After a few tries a hotel employee, who did not find her situation humorous, arrived to release her.

MUCHAS GRACIAS.

I'M SORRY I'M SO LATE!

OH, DON'T WORRY! WE WERE JUST DRAWING.

WE'VE GOT PLENTY OF TIME.

Miss Bell was gratified to have a story to tell.

YOU RAN DOWN AND UP AND DOWN THE FIFTEEN FLOORS OF STAIRS AND YOU'RE NOT EVEN WINDED?

THAT'S TRUE...

MUST BE THE COCA LEAVES!

# Saturday, September 21st

Miss Bell had to participate in a big panel called "Fighting the Blank Page."

THIS IS ANDRÉS BURGOS, HE WILL BE MODERATING YOUR PANEL.

I HEARD YOU ARE VERY SHY.

WHO TOLD YOU THAT? I'M NOT SHY!

It was the last day of the festival and everyone was tired of panels, but Miss Bell was out to prove she was not shy.

"WHAT IS YOUR BIGGEST CHALLENGE IN THE BATTLE WITH THE BLANK PAGE?"

INTERNET.

TEXTING.

THERE'S THIS WOODCHUCK WHO LIVES UNDER MY PORCH-I CALL HIM CHUCKLES-EVERY DAY HE GOES UNDER THE PEAR TREE IN THE YARD AND I WAIT WITH MY CAMERA TO GET A SHOT OF HIM WHEN HE GETS ON HIS HIND LEGS TO EAT A PEAR...

Miss Bell dominated the conversation, especially when she felt herself to be called upon to defend autobiography.

I MEAN...I TRY TO BRING OUT THE BEST IN PEOPLE...NOT TO SAY I'M GONNA PRESENT EVERYONE AS PERFECT...BUT I WON'T USE MY COMICS TO TAKE REVENGE ON ANYONE... ...UNLESS THEY DESERVE IT, HA HA.

On later reflection, Miss Bell would consider that one's personal experiences are the only things that one truly owns, and should need no defending.

"QUIERO DECIR...YO TRATO DE SACAR LO MEJOR DE LAS PERSONAS...ESTO NO SIGNIFICA QUE VOY A PRESENTAR A TODO EL MUNDO COMO SI FUERA PERFECTO... PERO NO USARÉ MIS CÓMICS PARA VENGARME DE NADIE... A NO SER QUE LO MEREZCAN, JA, JA."

Later there was a dance party.

Miss Bell leapt up and, in a burst of exhibitionism, performed an impromptu solo dance for her companions.

Mr. Gómez-Burns joined her, but she got shy and froze.

She retreated and Miss Braud got up and showed them how it was done.

Eventually, Miss Bell learned to salsa.

She also learned the tango.

But, as usual, failed at the robot.

Walking around Bogotá with Mr. Karlalopoulos, just before their departure, Miss Bell was fascinated by the street dogs.

HE LOOKS LIKE HE'S ON HIS WAY TO WORK...

I DON'T THINK SO. IT'S SUNDAY.

On a crowded intersection, they watched a poodle mix stand on its hind legs, take its owner's hand, and allow itself to be walked across the street.

When the two of them got to the other side, they'd linger a bit, turn around and cross again.

Miss Bell had an unpleasant flight home. She was placed at the back of the plane between two brutes who shamelessly encroached into her miniature slice of allotted space.

SNORE

Back in Brooklyn, she walks down the street, repeatedly struck by jarring, alternating bolts of joy and shame.

As for me, I am still in Bogotá, awaiting word from the American Embassy about a replacement for my stolen passport. In the meantime, I make a modest living training street dogs to perform tricks.

# Flight

chug
chug
chug

Hi, I'm on a plane. There's some turbulence. I don't mind, I'm just sitting here writing these words and working on my posture.

I've been reading the first chapter of <u>Zen Mind, Beginner's Mind</u>. It talks about correct posture in sitting zazen.

IF YOU SIT UP STRAIGHT, YOU ALREADY HAVE THE RIGHT STATE OF MIND, SO THERE IS NO NEED TO ATTAIN SOME SPECIAL STATE. IF YOU SLUMP, THE MIND WANDERS.

IS THAT ALL THERE IS TO IT?

YEP. THE STATE OF MIND THAT EXISTS WHEN YOU SIT IN THE RIGHT POSITION IS, IT-SELF, ENLIGHTEN-MENT.

He (Zen master Shunryu Suzuki) says you should try the correct posture while doing all activities, reading, driving a car, or drawing comics on a plane. The correct way is to keep your spine straight and your chin pulled in a little, as if you were supporting the sky with your head.

(SKY-HAT)

I've been trying to attain good posture all my life, but inevitably shame creeps in. And weariness. Resignation. Shame. Did I say shame twice? It's because I feel it twice as much. Shame at being so pretentious as to publicly attempt to better myself. Shame at my own existence.

And, oh man! What the hell is this? I've gotta pay for headphones AND movies!? It used to be the consolation for a packed, tiring flight was a trashy meal and a trashy movie. Now you expect me to pay for both of these? Nothing to do but read <u>Zen Mind, Beginner's Mind</u>.

...Or contemplate this man's head in front of me. His poor unfortun-ate head. There's a deep, craggy ravine through the top of it, and little scabs inside that he probably mindlessly scratches. And, insult to injury, a pathetic, brittle, greying little combover that doesn't even comb all the way over.

Then there's this flight attendant. We all know his name is Marc and that today is his birthday. Marc has a perfect head, perfect hair, perfect posture, his shirt tucked perfectly with no side bulges. Marc is the head flight attendant, in spite of being half the age of the other two.

But they don't seem to mind. They love Marc, even though he is young and beautiful and they are old.

EVERYBODY BE NICE TO OUR HEAD STEWARD MARC TODAY BECAUSE IT'S HIS BIRTHDAY.

I'm also getting side bulges but it's okay, I like them.

This little kid in the seat by the window in front of me has been singing the same lyric, whose meaning he couldn't possibly understand, of a pop song over and over since we've lifted off. Oh, little child, with your boundless, irrepressible joy, don't you know we can all hear you?

YOU GOT IT YOU GOT THAT BOOM-BOOM

And this guy across the aisle from me, the way he's tearing into that roast beef sandwich is shocking. It's weird and sexual. He has a look of desperation as he chews, as if this meal will save him. As for me, I've decided to forgo the salmon and egg sandwich I've packed.

Now here comes Marc, asking that kid:

WOULD YOU LIKE SOMETHING TO DRINK?

DO YOU HAVE ANY ICE CREAM?

HA HA, NO.

BUT I'LL BE RIGHT BACK.

Marc slips the boy, who is used to being rewarded for his cuteness, a special package.

THANK YOU.

KIDS BOX

The question is: how can I get Marc to bring a box for me?

Then there's this couple next to me. He's letting her use the earbuds for the wacky show they're watching on his iPhone. Her non-stop laughter sounds like gasping, or sobbing. She doesn't know how loud she is or how disturbing it sounds, and he is too kind, or too in love, to tell her.

SNORT!

The lady flight attendant flirts with the sandwich-eater. Why are these people being rewarded for their boorish behavior?

HOW WAS THE SAND-WICH? GOOD?

YEAH, CAN I GET A COFFEE? AM I TOO MUCH TROUBLE?

WHAD'YA WANT, A LATTE? A CAPPUCINO?

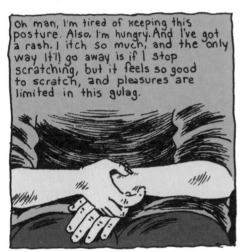

Oh man, I'm tired of keeping this posture. Also, I'm hungry. And I've got a rash. I itch so much, and the only way it'll go away is if I stop scratching, but it feels so good to scratch, and pleasures are limited in this gulag.

Oh, look, here's that kid.

GRAMPA, UM, I'M GONNA GO TO THE BATHROOM.

After awhile, I give in and break out my sandwich, chewing conscientiously.

This is why I like my side bulges. They are made of delicious things.

**Gabrielle Bell**'s work has been selected for the 2007, 2009-2013 Houghton-Mifflin *Best American Comics* and the *Yale Anthology of Graphic Fiction*, and has been featured in *McSweeney's*, *The Believer*, *Bookforum* and *Vice* magazines. The title story of her book "Cecil and Jordan In New York," was adapted for the screen by Bell and director Michel Gondry in the film anthology *Tokyo*! Her latest book, *The Voyeurs*, was selected as one of the top 5 Graphic Novels of 2012 by *Publishers Weekly*. She lives in Brooklyn.

Thank you Tom Kaczynski, Larry Livermore & everybody who allowed me to depict them in this book.